LOIRE VALLEY TRAVEL GUIDE

2023

Journey through the Loire Valley: Unveiling Hidden Gems, Local Traditions, and Unforgettable Experiences in the Heart of France

Ted Paul

TABLE OF CONTENT

Introduction

Welcome to the Loire Valley, a region of breathtaking beauty, rich history, and captivating culture. Nestled in the heart of France, this enchanting destination beckons travelers with its magnificent châteaux, rolling vineyards, and picturesque landscapes. Whether you're a history enthusiast, a wine lover, or simply seeking an escape into tranquility, the Loire Valley offers a diverse range of experiences to satisfy every traveler's desires.

In this comprehensive travel guide, we invite you to embark on a journey like no other—a journey through the secrets and wonders of the Loire Valley. Unveil the hidden gems, immerse yourself in local traditions, and create lasting memories as you explore this extraordinary region.

Chapter by chapter, we will guide you through the highlights and must-see attractions, providing you with insider tips and expert recommendations. Discover the iconic châteaux that grace the Loire Valley's landscape, from the majestic Château de Chambord, emerging from the wilderness with its awe-inspiring architecture, to the elegant Château de Chenonceau, gracefully spanning the River Cher with its timeless beauty. Learn about the fascinating histories and captivating stories that breathe life into these architectural marvels.

But the Loire Valley is more than just châteaux. Delve into the local traditions and gastronomic delights that make this region truly special. Indulge your senses in the flavors of the Loire Valley's renowned cuisine, from delectable dishes prepared with fresh local ingredients to the world-class wines that have made the region famous. Immerse yourself in the vibrant festivals and events that celebrate the rich cultural heritage of the Loire Valley, offering a glimpse into the traditions and customs that have shaped the region's identity.

Beyond the châteaux and traditions, the Loire Valley holds natural wonders waiting to be explored. Follow the meandering Loire River, the lifeline of the valley, as it leads you to stunning gardens and parks, providing moments of serenity amidst the beauty of nature. Engage in outdoor activities such as cycling or hiking along the riverbanks, immersing yourself in the captivating landscapes that have inspired artists and writers for centuries.

As you journey through the Loire Valley, we will also unveil the lesser-known treasures that lie off the beaten path. Discover quaint villages and historic towns that exude charm and authenticity, where rural life thrives and genuine encounters await. Venture into the hidden corners of the region, where you'll find hidden gems and unique experiences that will leave an indelible mark on your journey.

To ensure a seamless and enjoyable adventure, we provide practical information, insider tips, and resources to assist you in planning your trip. From the best time to visit to transportation options and accommodation recommendations, we've got you covered.

So, whether you're a first-time visitor or returning to rediscover the wonders of the Loire Valley, this travel guide will be your ultimate companion. Let us help you navigate this captivating region, uncover its treasures, and create unforgettable memories. Get ready to embark on a remarkable journey through the Loire Valley, where history, culture, and natural splendor await at every turn.

Overview of the Loire Valley Region

The Loire Valley, with its central location in France, captivates visitors with its unparalleled beauty and historical significance. Spanning approximately 280 kilometers (175 miles) along the majestic Loire River, this remarkable region is celebrated for its breathtaking landscapes, picturesque villages, and extraordinary cultural heritage. Its outstanding universal value has earned it the prestigious recognition as a UNESCO World Heritage site, showcasing its abundance of architectural treasures, idyllic vineyards, and natural wonders.

Often referred to as the "Garden of France," the Loire Valley boasts an enchanting ambiance characterized by lush greenery, vibrant floral displays, and fertile lands. The region showcases a remarkable diversity of landscapes that will leave visitors in awe. From rolling hills adorned with vineyards and orchards to expansive forests teeming with wildlife, from meandering rivers reflecting the surrounding beauty to fertile plains supporting bountiful agriculture, the Loire Valley's topography is a testament to the wonders of nature. This unique environment has proven to be ideal for viticulture, allowing the cultivation of exceptional grapes and the production of some of the world's most renowned wines.

However, it is the architectural splendors of the Loire Valley that truly capture the imagination. The region is home to an impressive array of châteaux, majestic castles, and opulent palaces that date back to the Renaissance and medieval periods. Each château showcases a harmonious blend of architectural styles, reflecting the diverse artistic influences that have shaped the region's history. From the soaring Gothic spires and intricate stone carvings to the elegant

Renaissance facades and grandiose Classical elements, these châteaux are a testament to the opulence and refined taste of French royalty and nobility throughout the centuries.

Each château in the Loire Valley has its own captivating story to tell. From the world-famous Château de Chambord, with its iconic double helix staircase and vast hunting grounds, to the exquisite Château de Chenonceau, gracefully spanning the Cher River with its delicate arches and stunning gardens, each architectural masterpiece offers a glimpse into the lives of the historical figures who once inhabited these magnificent structures. Visitors can wander through opulent chambers adorned with fine art and furnishings, stroll through meticulously manicured gardens, and immerse themselves in the opulence and splendor of a bygone era.

Beyond the châteaux, the Loire Valley is a tapestry of captivating towns and villages, each with its own distinct charm. Quaint cobblestone streets, half-timbered houses, and lively marketplaces create an inviting atmosphere where visitors can embrace the region's rich cultural heritage. Exploring these charming locales provides an opportunity to discover local traditions, taste regional delicacies, and engage with the warm and welcoming locals.

In conclusion, the Loire Valley is a destination that captivates the hearts and imaginations of all who visit. Its unparalleled beauty, remarkable cultural heritage, and architectural marvels make it a true gem in the heart of France. From the lush landscapes and vineyards to the grand châteaux that have withstood the test of time, the Loire Valley is a destination that leaves an indelible mark on every traveler fortunate enough to experience its wonders.

Why Visit the Loire Valley?

There are numerous reasons why the Loire Valley should be on every traveler's bucket list. Here are just a few compelling reasons to visit this enchanting region:

Rich History and Cultural Heritage:

The Loire Valley is a region deeply rooted in history, with a rich cultural heritage that spans thousands of years. Its story begins with ancient Roman settlements, evidence of which can still be seen today in the form of ruins and archaeological sites. The Romans recognized the strategic value of the Loire River and established towns and trade routes along its banks.

As the Middle Ages unfolded, the Loire Valley became a significant center of power and influence. Impressive fortresses and medieval castles were constructed to defend the region and assert the authority of feudal lords. These formidable structures, with their imposing ramparts and defensive features, offer a glimpse into the tumultuous times of knights, sieges, and feudalism.

However, it was during the Renaissance that the Loire Valley truly flourished as a hub of art, culture, and refined living. Influenced by the Italian Renaissance, French royalty and nobility constructed magnificent châteaux that showcased the wealth, elegance, and sophistication of the period. These architectural marvels became symbols of power and prestige, hosting lavish parties, courtly gatherings, and artistic pursuits.

Today, the Loire Valley stands as a living museum, inviting visitors to immerse themselves in the captivating stories and legends of the past. From exploring the remains of Roman settlements to admiring the architectural splendors of medieval fortresses and Renaissance castles, every step through the region's historic sites reveals a new chapter in its fascinating history.

Architectural Marvels:

The Loire Valley's châteaux are true architectural masterpieces, captivating visitors with their grandeur and timeless beauty. Each château showcases the finest craftsmanship and artistic expressions of its respective era, creating a tapestry of architectural styles that span centuries.

Visiting the Loire Valley's châteaux is like stepping into a fairy tale. The sight of turrets piercing the sky, expansive courtyards, and intricate details such as carved stone facades and ornate balconies evokes a sense of wonder and awe. The interiors are equally impressive, featuring lavish furnishings, exquisite artwork, and meticulously crafted decorations.

Château de Chambord, with its distinctive French Renaissance architecture, stands as a masterpiece of symmetry and elegance. Its double helix staircase is a marvel of engineering and remains a focal point of intrigue for visitors. Château de Chenonceau, spanning the Cher River, is a masterpiece of Renaissance and Gothic architecture, known as the "Ladies' Castle" due to its association with influential women throughout history. Château de Blois showcases a captivating blend of architectural styles, from its medieval fortress to its Renaissance wing, reflecting the evolution of architectural tastes over time.

Exploring these architectural gems is not only an opportunity to admire their beauty but also to gain insight into the lives of the noble families who once resided within their walls. With each visit, visitors can appreciate the architectural prowess and artistic vision that shaped the Loire Valley's landscape.

Natural Beauty:

The Loire Valley's natural beauty is an integral part of its charm. The region's landscape is characterized by the meandering Loire River, picturesque vineyards, and expansive forests, creating a haven for nature lovers.

The Loire River, often referred to as the "Royal River," is the backbone of the valley. Its tranquil waters wind through the countryside, providing a scenic backdrop for leisurely cruises and riverside walks. Along its banks, charming towns and villages offer glimpses of traditional life and architectural gems.

Vineyards are a prominent feature of the Loire Valley, producing a wide range of exceptional wines. The gently sloping hills are covered in meticulously tended vineyards, offering a stunning sight, particularly during the harvest season. Wine enthusiasts can indulge in wine tastings, vineyard tours, and even take part in grape harvesting experiences, immersing themselves in the winemaking traditions of the region.

The Loire Valley's expansive forests, such as the Forest of Amboise and the Forest of Chinon, add to its natural allure. These wooded areas are a haven for wildlife and provide opportunities for hiking, cycling, and picnicking amidst the serene beauty of nature. The forests also play a crucial role in preserving the region's biodiversity, housing diverse plant species and serving as habitats for various animal species.

Gardens and parks are abundant throughout the Loire Valley, offering enchanting spaces for relaxation and contemplation. From meticulously manicured formal gardens to whimsical English-style landscapes, each garden holds its own unique charm. Visitors can wander through fragrant rose gardens, stroll along tree-lined avenues, and admire ornate fountains and sculptures that dot the landscape.

The combination of the Loire River, vineyards, forests, and gardens creates a harmonious blend of natural beauty that sets the stage for a peaceful and rejuvenating experience. Whether it's a leisurely bike ride along the riverbanks, a picnic in a charming park, or a hike through the forest trails, the Loire Valley invites visitors to reconnect with nature and find solace in its tranquil surroundings.

Gastronomic Delights:

The Loire Valley is a gastronomic paradise, offering a delightful culinary journey for food and wine enthusiasts. The region's fertile lands and diverse terroir provide the perfect conditions for producing a wide array of fresh and flavorful ingredients.

One of the culinary highlights of the Loire Valley is its exceptional wines. The region is renowned for its white wines, such as Sancerre, Pouilly-Fumé, and Vouvray, which are celebrated for their elegance, complexity, and ability to express the unique characteristics of the terroir. Red wines, including Chinon and Bourgueil, offer rich and robust flavors, while the sparkling wines of Saumur and Crémant de Loire add a touch of effervescence to any celebration.

In addition to its wines, the Loire Valley boasts a diverse culinary heritage. Local specialties include rillettes, a delicious spread made from slow-cooked pork, and goat cheese, such as Crottin de Chavignol, known for its distinct flavor and creamy texture. The region's freshwater rivers and streams provide an abundance of fish, such as pike, perch, and trout, which are often featured in traditional dishes.

Exploring the Loire Valley's gastronomy is a treat for the senses. From charming local restaurants serving classic dishes to Michelin-starred establishments pushing the boundaries of culinary creativity, there are endless opportunities to indulge in the flavors of the region. Traditional markets, filled with vibrant fruits, vegetables, cheeses, and artisanal products, offer a chance to engage with local producers and discover the true essence of Loire Valley cuisine.

The combination of exceptional wines, flavorful dishes, and a commitment to culinary excellence make the Loire Valley a true epicurean destination, where every meal is an opportunity to savor the region's gastronomic delights.

In summary, the Loire Valley entices visitors with its rich history, architectural marvels, natural beauty, and gastronomic treasures. It is a region that encapsulates the essence of France, offering a captivating journey through time, an immersion in architectural splendors, a tranquil escape into nature, and a culinary adventure that delights the taste buds. Whether exploring ancient Roman settlements, admiring the grandeur of châteaux, meandering along the riverbanks, or indulging in the flavors of the region, the Loire Valley promises an unforgettable experience that combines culture, beauty, and culinary delights.

Practical Information and Travel Tips

Before embarking on your Loire Valley adventure, it is essential to be well-prepared. Here are some practical tips and information to help you make the most of your visit:

Best Time to Visit:

The Loire Valley is beautiful year-round, but the best time to visit depends on your preferences. Here's a more detailed exploration of each season:

Spring and Early Summer (April to June):

Spring is a delightful time to visit the Loire Valley as the region emerges from the cold grip of winter and nature begins to awaken. The weather during spring is generally mild and pleasant, making it an ideal time to explore the outdoor wonders of the valley. Temperatures typically range from around 10°C to 20°C (50°F to 68°F), creating a comfortable atmosphere for outdoor activities and sightseeing.

One of the highlights of spring in the Loire Valley is the explosion of blooming flowers that blanket the landscapes. As you traverse the countryside, you'll be treated to a vibrant display of colors. Tulips, daffodils, and cherry blossoms burst into bloom, painting the fields and gardens with their vivid hues. The sight of these delicate and fragrant flowers is truly enchanting and adds a touch of magic to the already picturesque scenery.

In addition to the floral extravaganza, spring in the Loire Valley offers the advantage of fewer crowds compared to the peak summer months. This means you'll have more space and tranquility to explore the region's famous châteaux, charming towns, and scenic landscapes. You can take your time admiring the architectural marvels, strolling through the manicured gardens, and immersing yourself in the history and culture of the area without feeling rushed or crowded.

Springtime also presents the opportunity to witness the Loire Valley's vineyards coming to life. The vineyards, which produce some of the finest wines in France, start to bud and show signs of the forthcoming grape harvest. Wine enthusiasts can take advantage of this time to visit the wineries, learn about the winemaking process, and perhaps even participate in tastings and cellar tours.

Furthermore, spring in the Loire Valley offers pleasant conditions for outdoor activities. You can embark on leisurely bike rides along the Loire River, meandering through charming villages and vineyards. The mild temperatures and blossoming landscapes create an idyllic setting for picnics in the countryside or riverside walks, allowing you to fully immerse yourself in the region's natural beauty.

In summary, spring is an ideal time to visit the Loire Valley. The mild and pleasant weather, the vibrant blooming flowers, and the fewer crowds create an atmosphere of tranquility and beauty. Whether you are an admirer of nature, a history enthusiast, or a wine lover, springtime in the Loire Valley offers a perfect blend of natural wonders and cultural treasures, making it a truly delightful season to explore this enchanting region.

Summer (July and August):

Summer is indeed the peak tourist season in the Loire Valley, attracting visitors from around the world who are eager to experience the region's splendor under the warm sun. Here's a more detailed exploration of what makes summer a popular time to visit, along with some considerations:

Weather and Outdoor Activities:

During summer, the Loire Valley experiences warm and sunny weather, with temperatures averaging between 20°C and 30°C (68°F to 86°F). This pleasant climate creates an ideal setting for a wide range of outdoor activities. Visitors can explore the châteaux and their magnificent gardens at a leisurely pace, taking in the sights and enjoying the manicured landscapes. The long daylight hours provide ample time for extended exploration, and it's particularly magical to witness the châteaux illuminated in the evening, adding a touch of enchantment to your visit.

Picnics and Riverside Relaxation:

Summer offers the perfect opportunity to indulge in picnics along the Loire River or its tributaries. Pack a basket filled with local delicacies, such as cheese, baguettes, and fresh fruits, and find a scenic spot to enjoy a leisurely meal while surrounded by the serene beauty of the river and the picturesque countryside. The riverbanks also provide a peaceful setting for a stroll, a bike ride, or even a boat trip, allowing you to immerse yourself in the tranquility and natural splendor of the region.

Vibrant Festivals and Events:

Summer in the Loire Valley is synonymous with vibrant festivals and cultural events. The region comes alive with celebrations, concerts, and performances that showcase the rich heritage and artistic traditions of the area. From music festivals held in historic châteaux to lively street fairs and wine tastings, there is always something happening during the summer months. These events offer a unique opportunity to mingle with locals, immerse yourself in the cultural fabric of the region, and create unforgettable memories.

Considerations:

a. Crowds: It's important to note that summer is the busiest time of the year in the Loire Valley, and popular tourist sites can become quite crowded. If you prefer a quieter and more intimate experience, it may be worth planning your visit during shoulder seasons like spring or autumn when there are fewer tourists.

b. Higher Prices: As summer attracts a large number of visitors, prices for accommodations, dining, and tourist attractions tend to be higher during this season. It is advisable to book your accommodations well in advance to secure your preferred options and consider budgeting accordingly.

c. Reservations: To make the most of your visit during the summer months, it is recommended to make reservations for popular châteaux tours, events, and restaurants in advance. This will help ensure you have access to the attractions and experiences you desire without facing disappointment due to limited availability.

By considering these factors, you can plan your summer visit to the Loire Valley with realistic expectations and make the necessary arrangements to enjoy the region's natural beauty, cultural events, and warm weather to the fullest extent possible

Autumn (September to October):

Autumn in the Loire Valley is a season that captivates the senses with its breathtaking beauty. As the temperatures begin to cool down, ranging from 10°C to 20°C (50°F to 68°F), the region enjoys a comfortable and pleasant climate for outdoor activities. The moderate weather invites visitors to explore the stunning landscapes and engage in various pursuits while appreciating the transformative colors of nature.

One of the most remarkable aspects of autumn in the Loire Valley is the transformation of the countryside. As the leaves of the region's abundant trees start to change, the landscape becomes a vibrant mosaic of red, orange, and gold. The charming châteaux, nestled amidst this kaleidoscope of colors, appear even more picturesque against the backdrop of the changing foliage. Photographers find themselves immersed in a paradise of stunning compositions, capturing the beauty of nature in its most captivating form.

Nature lovers are drawn to the Loire Valley during autumn for the opportunity to witness the region's stunning landscapes and picturesque scenes. The forests and vineyards, which cover vast expanses of the valley, are particularly enchanting during this season. Walking along the scenic trails and meandering through the vineyard-dotted countryside becomes a sensory experience, with the crisp air carrying the scent of fallen leaves and the earthy aroma of the harvest.

Autumn is also the grape harvest season in the Loire Valley, adding another layer of charm and excitement to the region. Vineyards come alive with activity as winemakers and farmers work diligently to gather the ripe grapes. This period offers a unique opportunity for visitors to participate in wine-related events and tastings, immersing themselves in the rich winemaking traditions of the region. From strolling through vineyards and witnessing the harvest process to sampling the finest wines produced during this time, visitors can engage in a sensory journey that celebrates the culmination of a year's worth of labor and the fruits of the land.

The Loire Valley embraces autumn with open arms, inviting travelers to revel in the region's extraordinary beauty and experience the richness of its cultural and natural heritage. Whether it's capturing the vibrant colors of the changing leaves, embarking on wine-related adventures, or simply enjoying the comfortable weather while exploring the châteaux and countryside, autumn offers an unforgettable and enchanting experience for all who visit.

Winter (November to February):

Winter brings a unique charm to the Loire Valley, transforming it into a winter wonderland. Although temperatures can be cold, ranging from 0°C to 10°C (32°F to 50°F), the region embraces a tranquil and magical atmosphere that captivates visitors.

One of the highlights of winter in the Loire Valley is the opportunity to stay in the château hotels. These grand estates offer a truly enchanting experience during the colder months. Imagine stepping into a fairytale as you enter the historic halls adorned with elegant decorations and sparkling lights. The crackling fireplaces create a cozy ambiance, inviting guests to relax and unwind in luxurious surroundings. Curling up with a good book or sipping a glass of local wine by the fire becomes a cherished memory.

Winter is also a time to indulge in hearty meals that warm the soul. The region's renowned gastronomy shines during this season, with restaurants offering comforting dishes such as foie gras, coq au vin, and hearty stews. Local wineries showcase their robust red wines, perfectly paired with the rich flavors of the cuisine. The combination of exquisite food, fine wine, and the charming ambiance of a winter evening creates a culinary experience to savor.

One of the highlights of the winter season in the Loire Valley is the abundance of Christmas markets. These festive markets, scattered throughout the region, offer a delightful immersion into the holiday spirit. Stroll through the market stalls adorned with twinkling lights, and browse the array of locally crafted goods, including handmade ornaments, pottery, textiles, and artisanal foods. The aromas of mulled wine, roasted chestnuts, and gingerbread fill the air, enticing visitors to sample the seasonal treats. Traditional carols and live performances add to the joyful atmosphere, creating a magical experience for all ages.

Winter also provides the opportunity to explore the region's rich cultural heritage. Many of the châteaux remain open during this season, and the reduced number of visitors allows for a more intimate and personal experience. Imagine walking through the halls of the grand castles, admiring their magnificent architecture and priceless artworks without the hustle and bustle of peak tourist times. The tranquility of winter allows visitors to appreciate the intricate details of these historical landmarks and connect with their captivating stories on a deeper level.

Whether you choose to immerse yourself in the cozy ambiance of the château hotels, indulge in hearty meals by crackling fireplaces, explore the enchanting Christmas markets, or simply soak in the tranquil beauty of the region, the Loire Valley in winter offers a unique and memorable experience. It's a time to embrace the holiday spirit, create cherished memories, and appreciate the captivating charm of this remarkable destination.

Overall, the Loire Valley offers something special in every season. Whether you prefer the blooming beauty of spring, the lively festivities of summer, the vibrant colors of autumn, or the tranquil charm of winter, the region's diverse attractions and cultural heritage are sure to leave a lasting impression, regardless of the time you choose to visit.

Getting There:

The Loire Valley is easily accessible from major cities in France. The closest international airports are in Paris, namely Charles de Gaulle Airport and Orly Airport, both of which are well-connected to various destinations around the world. If you are arriving from outside of France, flying into one of these airports is a convenient option to begin your journey to the Loire Valley.

From Paris, you have several transportation options to reach the Loire Valley. One of the most popular and convenient methods is by train. The French railway network, operated by SNCF, offers frequent and efficient train services from Paris to various cities and towns in the Loire Valley. The journey duration typically ranges from one to two hours, depending on your specific destination within the region. Trains depart from Paris' major train stations, including Gare Montparnasse, Gare d'Austerlitz, and Gare de Lyon.

Renting a car is another popular option for exploring the Loire Valley at your own pace and flexibility. If you prefer to have the freedom to visit multiple châteaux, picturesque villages, and off-the-beaten-path attractions, renting a car provides convenience and allows you to create your own itinerary. Several car rental companies have offices at the airports and major cities, offering a range of vehicle options to suit your needs. The journey from Paris to the Loire Valley by car usually takes around two to three hours, depending on traffic and your specific destination within the region.

Additionally, private transportation services, such as taxis or chauffeured cars, can be arranged for a more personalized and comfortable travel experience. These services can be pre-booked to ensure a smooth transfer from Paris to the Loire Valley, and they provide the convenience of door-to-door transportation.

In addition to the options mentioned above, there are a few more ways to reach the Loire Valley from major cities in France:

High-Speed Trains (TGV):

France's high-speed train network, the TGV (Train à Grande Vitesse), is an excellent option for travelers coming from major cities across the country. Cities like Lyon, Marseille, Nantes, and Bordeaux have direct TGV connections to various destinations in the Loire Valley. These trains offer a comfortable and time-efficient mode of transportation, allowing you to reach the Loire Valley quickly and conveniently.

The TGV trains provide a high level of comfort with spacious seating, onboard amenities, and a smooth and quiet ride. They are known for their punctuality and efficiency, making them an ideal choice for those who prioritize speed and convenience. The journey on a TGV from major cities to the Loire Valley can range from around one to three hours, depending on the distance and specific destination.

Regional Trains:

If you are already in a city or town near the Loire Valley, regional trains are a convenient option for traveling within the region. SNCF operates regional train services that connect smaller towns and cities within the Loire Valley. While these trains may take slightly longer than high-speed trains, they offer a more localized travel experience, allowing you to explore smaller towns and discover hidden gems off the beaten path.

Regional trains provide a comfortable and scenic journey, with panoramic windows that offer picturesque views of the countryside. They are a great way to soak in the charm and beauty of the Loire Valley while traveling between towns like Tours, Angers, Blois, Saumur, and Amboise. These trains also offer flexibility in terms of departure times and ticket options, making them a convenient choice for spontaneous travelers.

Bus Services:

For budget-conscious travelers or those seeking alternative transportation options, several bus companies operate routes connecting the Loire Valley to major cities and towns in France. These buses offer an affordable way to travel and can be a good choice for those who prefer a more flexible schedule.

While bus travel may take longer than trains, it provides an opportunity to enjoy the scenic landscapes and rural beauty of the Loire Valley. The bus routes often include stops at key towns and attractions, allowing you to explore the region at your own pace. However, it's important to note that bus services may have fewer departure options compared to trains, so it's advisable to check the schedules in advance and plan accordingly.

River Cruises:

For a unique and leisurely way to reach the Loire Valley, consider a river cruise along the Loire River itself. River cruises offer a truly immersive experience, allowing you to enjoy the natural beauty of the riverbanks, picturesque landscapes, and charming villages as you make your way to the heart of the Loire Valley.

River cruises often have dedicated itineraries that include stops at key towns and attractions along the Loire River, such as Nantes, Angers, Saumur, and Tours. These cruises provide an opportunity to explore the region's rich cultural heritage, sample local wines, and indulge in the gastronomic delights of the Loire Valley. They offer a relaxed and scenic journey, with onboard amenities, guided tours, and the expertise of knowledgeable guides to enhance your experience.

When planning your journey to the Loire Valley, consider factors such as travel time, convenience, cost, and personal preferences. It's recommended to check the schedules and availability of different transportation options in advance, especially during peak travel seasons. By selecting the most suitable mode of transportation, you can begin your exploration of the Loire Valley with ease, setting the stage for an immersive and memorable travel experience.

Getting Around:

The Loire Valley offers several options for getting around and exploring its attractions and charming towns.

Car Rental:

Renting a car is a popular choice for many travelers visiting the Loire Valley due to the flexibility and convenience it offers. The region has a well-developed network of roads, ranging from major highways to smaller scenic routes, making it relatively easy to navigate and explore.

One of the main advantages of renting a car is the freedom it provides to explore remote areas and venture off the beaten path. While public transportation options like trains and buses are available in the region, they may not reach all the hidden gems and lesser-known attractions that are scattered throughout the Loire Valley. Having a car allows you to discover these hidden treasures at your own pace, offering a sense of adventure and the opportunity to create your own unique itinerary.

With a rental car, you have the flexibility to visit multiple châteaux and attractions in the Loire Valley without being bound by strict schedules. You can plan your own route, choose the order in which you visit different sites, and spend as much time as you desire at each location. This allows for a more personalized and immersive experience, as you can fully immerse yourself in the history, architecture, and natural beauty of each place you visit.

Car rental agencies can be found at major airports, train stations, and in larger towns within the Loire Valley. It is advisable to book your rental car in advance, especially during peak travel seasons, to ensure availability and secure the best rates. Rental agencies offer a variety of vehicle options to suit different needs and budgets, ranging from compact cars to larger vehicles that can accommodate families or groups of travelers.

Before embarking on your journey, it's essential to familiarize yourself with local driving regulations and road signs. In France, cars drive on the right-hand side of the road, and speed limits vary depending on the type of road. It's also important to note that some older towns and city centers in the Loire Valley may have narrow streets and limited parking options, so it's advisable to plan accordingly and research parking facilities in advance.

Overall, renting a car in the Loire Valley provides the freedom, convenience, and flexibility to explore the region's enchanting landscapes, visit châteaux, and discover hidden gems. It allows you to craft your own unique adventure and make the most of your time in this captivating part of France.

Public Transportation:

The Loire Valley benefits from a well-developed transportation system that caters to the needs of travelers looking to explore the region's diverse attractions. Here are the various modes of transportation available:

1. Trains:

The Loire Valley benefits from an extensive and efficient train network, allowing travelers to easily access major cities and towns within the region and connect with other parts of France. One of the key features of the train system in the Loire Valley is the "Train à Grande Vitesse" (TGV), which is the high-speed train network in France.

The TGV provides a rapid and convenient way to reach the Loire Valley from various locations, including Paris and other major cities across the country. This high-speed train service offers a comfortable and enjoyable travel experience. The spacious seating ensures ample legroom and comfort, allowing passengers to relax during their journey. Additionally, the TGV is equipped with onboard amenities, such as power outlets and Wi-Fi, enabling travelers to stay connected or work while en route.

One of the highlights of traveling by train in the Loire Valley is the opportunity to enjoy scenic views of the picturesque countryside. As the train speeds through the region, passengers are treated to captivating vistas of rolling hills, vineyards, charming villages, and the serene Loire River. The large windows of the train carriages provide panoramic views, creating a truly immersive and memorable journey.

The train stations in the Loire Valley are well-equipped to cater to the needs of travelers. They offer a range of facilities and services to ensure a smooth and enjoyable experience. At the stations, visitors will find ticket counters where they can purchase tickets or seek assistance from knowledgeable staff. Information centers are also available, providing valuable resources, maps, and travel advice to help visitors plan their itineraries effectively. The stations serve as transportation hubs, connecting travelers to regional train services that link smaller towns and villages within the Loire Valley. This enables visitors to explore the region comprehensively, reaching not only major cities but also lesser-known gems.

Overall, traveling by train in the Loire Valley offers a combination of convenience, comfort, and scenic beauty. It allows visitors to efficiently navigate the region, providing access to its captivating attractions, including the world-famous châteaux, while offering a pleasant and memorable travel experience. Whether embarking on a day trip or an extended exploration of the Loire Valley, the train system serves as a reliable and enjoyable mode of transportation for both domestic and international travelers.

2. Buses:

Public buses in the Loire Valley offer an affordable and convenient means of transportation for travelers wishing to explore the region's diverse attractions. These buses provide vital connections between towns and villages, ensuring that visitors can easily access various points of interest, including smaller châteaux and off-the-beaten-path locations that may not have direct train connections.

The bus routes are thoughtfully designed to cater to the needs of both locals and tourists. They are strategically planned to encompass key tourist destinations, allowing visitors to navigate the region and explore its cultural and natural treasures. Whether you're looking to visit renowned châteaux like Château de Chambord or discover hidden gems tucked away in the countryside, the bus network provides access to a wide range of attractions.

To assist travelers in planning their journeys, comprehensive information regarding bus timetables, routes, and fares can be easily obtained from various sources. Tourist information centers, conveniently located in many towns and cities, serve as valuable resources where visitors can obtain brochures, maps, and schedules. Bus stations also provide up-to-date information, with staff available to answer questions and provide assistance. Additionally, online resources such as official bus company websites and travel planning platforms offer detailed information on bus services, making it convenient to research and plan your itinerary in advance.

Opting for buses in the Loire Valley not only offers affordability but also flexibility. With a well-connected network, travelers have the freedom to tailor their trips according to their preferences and interests. Buses often follow scenic routes, winding through picturesque countryside and offering panoramic views of vineyards, rolling hills, and charming villages. This allows passengers to immerse themselves in the region's natural beauty while en route to their desired destinations.

Moreover, buses offer a social aspect to travel, providing opportunities to interact with locals and fellow tourists. Onboard, you can engage in conversations, exchange travel tips, and learn more about the region from fellow passengers. The relaxed atmosphere of bus travel allows you to absorb the local ambiance and gain insights into the Loire Valley's culture and way of life.

By utilizing the Loire Valley's public bus system, travelers can enjoy a budget-friendly and flexible mode of transportation that connects them to the region's rich historical and cultural heritage. Whether you're venturing to well-known landmarks or venturing off the beaten path, buses offer an accessible and scenic way to explore the enchanting landscapes and discover the hidden gems of the Loire Valley.

3. Taxis:

In larger towns and cities within the Loire Valley, such as Tours, Orléans, and Blois, taxis are readily available, offering a convenient mode of transportation for both locals and tourists. Taxis provide a reliable and flexible option for reaching specific destinations or traveling shorter distances within the region.

When in need of a taxi, you can typically find them at designated taxi stands or hailed on the street. In busier areas, such as train stations or major attractions, you are likely to find a line of taxis waiting for passengers. Additionally, many towns and cities have taxi companies that can be contacted for booking a taxi in advance. This can be particularly useful during peak travel seasons or when you have specific time constraints.

To ensure transparency and avoid any surprises, it is advisable to inquire about fares or ask for an estimate before starting your journey. Taxi drivers are generally happy to provide an estimate based on your destination or distance. Additionally, most taxis have a meter that calculates the fare based on the distance traveled and the duration of the journey. It is common for taxi drivers to display the fare chart inside the vehicle, which indicates the starting fare and additional charges for waiting time or luggage.

One of the key advantages of using taxis in the Loire Valley is the convenience of a door-to-door service. Taxis offer a direct transportation option, allowing travelers to reach their desired locations with ease and efficiency. Whether you need to visit a specific château, explore a charming village, or reach your accommodation, taxis can take you directly to your destination without the need for transfers or navigating public transportation.

Taxis are particularly useful when exploring areas with limited public transportation options. Some smaller châteaux or off-the-beaten-path attractions may not have direct bus or train connections. In such cases, taxis provide a convenient solution, ensuring you can reach these destinations without difficulty. Additionally, if you are traveling with heavy luggage or have mobility concerns, taxis offer a comfortable and hassle-free way to travel.

Overall, taxis in the Loire Valley provide a reliable, convenient, and efficient mode of transportation, especially within larger towns and cities. By utilizing taxi services, you can enjoy the flexibility to travel on your schedule, reach specific destinations with ease, and navigate the region comfortably.

Château Shuttle Services:

Château Shuttle Services are a convenient transportation option provided by many of the popular châteaux in the Loire Valley. These shuttle services aim to make it easier for visitors to access the châteaux and explore the surrounding areas without the need for a car or relying on public transportation.

The shuttle services typically operate between nearby towns, train stations, and the châteaux themselves, ensuring that visitors have seamless access to these iconic landmarks. They are especially beneficial for tourists who may not have their own means of transportation or prefer not to drive during their visit.

To make use of the château shuttle services, it is advisable to check the specific château's website or inquire at the local tourist office for detailed information about shuttle schedules and pick-up points. The château websites often provide up-to-date information on the shuttle service, including departure times, frequency, and any associated fees.

By using the shuttle services, visitors can enjoy a hassle-free journey to the châteaux, saving time and effort in navigating unfamiliar roads or dealing with parking. It also allows them to relax and fully immerse themselves in the beauty of the Loire Valley without the distractions of driving.

Additionally, the shuttle services offer the added benefit of providing commentary or informative guides during the journey. This allows visitors to learn more about the history, architecture, and significance of the châteaux and the surrounding region, enhancing their overall experience.

The shuttle services may also include additional stops at points of interest or attractions along the way, providing an opportunity to explore the local area beyond the château itself. This can include visits to charming villages, local markets, or other notable landmarks, further enriching the visitor's understanding and appreciation of the Loire Valley.

It is important to note that shuttle schedules and availability may vary depending on the season and specific château. During peak tourist periods, such as summer, it is recommended to plan ahead and consider making reservations or arriving early to secure a seat on the shuttle.

In conclusion, the château shuttle services in the Loire Valley offer a convenient and efficient means of transportation for visitors to access the renowned châteaux and explore the surrounding areas. By checking the specific château's website or contacting the local tourist office for information, visitors can ensure a smooth and enjoyable experience, allowing them to fully immerse themselves in the rich history and architectural wonders of the Loire Valley.

Walking:

Walking is a delightful and immersive way to experience the beauty and charm of the Loire Valley. The region's scenic landscapes, picturesque villages, and historic sites lend themselves perfectly to exploration on foot.

One of the advantages of walking in the Loire Valley is the accessibility of certain attractions. For example, the famous Château de Chenonceau is within walking distance from train stations or nearby towns. This allows visitors to easily reach the château without the need for additional transportation. The leisurely walk to Chenonceau can be a scenic experience in itself, as you meander through charming countryside or along the banks of the Loire River.

Moreover, many towns in the Loire Valley boast well-preserved historic centers, inviting visitors to take leisurely strolls through their narrow streets. These historic centers are often pedestrian-friendly, with limited vehicle access, creating a peaceful and intimate ambiance. As you walk through these towns, you can immerse yourself in the local atmosphere, discovering hidden alleys, quaint cafés, and charming boutiques. The architecture of the buildings showcases the region's rich history, with timber-framed houses, cobblestone streets, and architectural details that transport you back in time.

While walking in the Loire Valley, you may come across small, off-the-beaten-path attractions that are not as widely known but hold their own unique charm. These hidden gems can surprise and delight, offering unexpected encounters with local artisans, artisans, or breathtaking viewpoints of the surrounding landscapes. Walking allows you to be more spontaneous and open to these serendipitous discoveries

In addition to the physical and cultural aspects, walking in the Loire Valley also offers a chance to connect with nature. The region's diverse landscapes, including the Loire River, vineyards, and rolling hills, provide a picturesque backdrop as you wander along designated paths and trails. You can appreciate the tranquility and beauty of the surroundings, pausing to observe the wildlife, enjoy a picnic in a scenic spot, or simply take in the sights and sounds of nature.

To make the most of your walking experiences in the Loire Valley, it is recommended to wear comfortable shoes, dress appropriately for the weather, and carry a map or guidebook to navigate your way. Local tourist offices can provide information on walking routes, trail maps, and any specific points of interest along the way. By embracing the slower pace of walking, you can fully immerse yourself in the region's beauty, uncover hidden gems, and create lasting memories of your time in the Loire Valley.

Cycling:

Cycling in the Loire Valley provides an immersive and unforgettable experience, allowing visitors to connect with the region's breathtaking landscapes, charming towns, and vineyard-dotted countryside. Renowned as one of the most cyclist-friendly regions in France, the Loire Valley offers a well-developed network of dedicated cycling paths known as "La Loire à Vélo" (The Loire by Bike).

Covering over 800 kilometers (500 miles) of carefully marked routes, La Loire à Vélo follows the course of the Loire River, meandering through picturesque towns, lush vineyards, and rolling countryside. The cycling paths are designed to be safe, scenic, and easily navigable, catering to cyclists of all levels, from casual riders to experienced enthusiasts. The routes are mostly flat, making them accessible and enjoyable for riders of all ages and fitness levels.

One of the main advantages of cycling in the Loire Valley is the opportunity to explore at your own pace. Renting bicycles from various rental shops is a popular option, with a wide range of bikes available, including hybrid bikes, mountain bikes, and electric bikes. Rental shops can be found in major towns along the cycling routes, making it convenient to start and end your cycling adventure.

For those seeking a more structured experience, guided cycling tours are also available. These tours provide an expert guide who leads the way, offering insights into the region's history, culture, and natural wonders. Guided tours often include visits to renowned châteaux, wine tastings at local vineyards, and opportunities to savor regional cuisine.

As you cycle through the Loire Valley, you'll be immersed in its stunning natural beauty. The cycling paths wind through lush forests, vineyards blanketed with grapevines, and along the banks of the serene Loire River. Along the way, you'll encounter charming towns and villages that invite you to take a break and explore their cobbled streets, historic landmarks, and local shops. Quaint cafes and restaurants provide opportunities to indulge in regional delicacies, savoring the flavors of the Loire Valley's renowned gastronomy.

In addition to the scenic beauty and cultural delights, cycling in the Loire Valley offers the chance to witness the region's rich biodiversity. The area is home to several nature reserves and protected areas, providing habitats for a diverse range of wildlife. Birdwatchers will be delighted by the opportunity to spot herons, kingfishers, and other avian species that thrive in the wetlands along the Loire River.

Safety is a top priority for cycling enthusiasts, and the Loire Valley takes this seriously. The cycling paths are well-maintained, with clear signage and dedicated lanes, ensuring a safe and enjoyable ride. Along the routes, you'll find cyclist-friendly amenities such as repair stations, rest areas, and bike-friendly accommodations.

Whether you choose to embark on a solo cycling adventure or join a guided tour, exploring the Loire Valley by bike allows you to connect intimately with the region's landscapes, heritage, and local culture. It provides a unique perspective and a sense of freedom as you pedal through vineyards, pass by majestic châteaux, and take in the idyllic scenery of this enchanting region.

Whether you prefer the speed and comfort of trains, the affordability and flexibility of buses, or the convenience of taxis, the Loire Valley's transportation options cater to various travel preferences. By utilizing these modes of transportation, visitors can seamlessly navigate the region, discovering its captivating châteaux, picturesque towns, and scenic landscapes while experiencing the convenience and efficiency of the transportation network.

Accommodation:

The Loire Valley offers a range of accommodation options to suit every budget and preference. From luxury château hotels and charming bed and breakfasts to cozy guesthouses and campgrounds, there is something for everyone. It is advisable to book your accommodation in advance, especially during peak travel seasons.

When it comes to finding accommodation in the Loire Valley, visitors are spoiled for choice. The region is known for its exquisite château hotels, where guests can immerse themselves in the opulent ambiance of centuries-old castles. These luxury accommodations offer an unforgettable experience, with elegant rooms, fine dining, and impeccable service. Staying in a château hotel allows you to live like royalty, surrounded by stunning architecture and lavish gardens.

For those seeking a more intimate and personalized experience, bed and breakfasts are an excellent option. The Loire Valley is dotted with charming B&Bs, often located in historic buildings or traditional country houses. These accommodations provide a cozy and welcoming atmosphere, with comfortable rooms and homemade breakfasts that showcase the region's local flavors.

Guesthouses, or "chambres d'hôtes," are another popular choice in the Loire Valley. These accommodations are typically run by local residents who open their homes to guests. Staying in a guesthouse allows you to interact with friendly hosts, who can provide insider tips on the best places to visit and hidden gems to explore. It's a wonderful opportunity to experience the warmth and hospitality of the region.

For travelers on a tighter budget or those seeking a more rustic experience, campgrounds are available throughout the Loire Valley. These campsites offer a chance to immerse yourself in nature, surrounded by lush landscapes and tranquil settings. Whether you prefer pitching a tent or staying in a mobile home, campgrounds provide a cost-effective and adventurous accommodation option.

Regardless of the type of accommodation you choose, it is advisable to book in advance, especially during the peak travel seasons of spring and summer. The Loire Valley attracts visitors from all over the world, and popular accommodations can fill up quickly. Booking in advance ensures that you secure your desired lodging and allows you to plan your itinerary with peace of mind.

When selecting your accommodation, consider the location in relation to the attractions you wish to visit. Some châteaux have their own on-site accommodations, allowing you to fully immerse yourself in the castle experience. Others are located in nearby towns or villages, providing a charming and convenient base for exploring the region. Take into account factors such as proximity to public transportation, dining options, and the overall ambiance you desire.

In addition to considering the type and location of accommodation, it's important to keep a few other factors in mind when booking your stay in the Loire Valley.

Firstly, consider the duration of your visit. The region offers a wealth of attractions, including numerous châteaux, vineyards, and natural landscapes. If you plan to explore the area extensively, you might want to consider booking accommodations in different locations to minimize travel time and maximize your experience. This way, you can strategically choose accommodations that are closer to the specific attractions you wish to visit, saving you time and allowing for more flexibility in your itinerary.

Another important consideration is the amenities and services offered by the accommodation. Make a list of your priorities and preferences, such as Wi-Fi access, on-site parking, dining options, or leisure facilities. If you're traveling with children, you might want to look for accommodations that cater to families, offering amenities like playgrounds or family-friendly activities. Similarly, if you have accessibility needs, ensure that the accommodation you choose provides the necessary facilities or assistance.

Reviews and recommendations from previous guests can provide valuable insights into the quality and service of the accommodations you are considering. Check online review platforms or travel websites to read about the experiences of other travelers. Look for feedback regarding cleanliness, comfort, staff friendliness, and any specific aspects that are important to you. These reviews can help you make an informed decision and avoid any potential surprises.

Lastly, don't forget to consider the additional services and experiences that your chosen accommodation might offer. Some château hotels organize guided tours of their premises, wine tastings, or special events that provide a deeper understanding of the region's heritage. Bed and breakfasts might offer cooking classes or organize visits to local markets. Exploring these additional offerings can enhance your overall experience and provide unique insights into the local culture and traditions.

By taking these factors into account and conducting thorough research, you can find the perfect accommodation that suits your preferences, budget, and travel plans in the Loire Valley. Whether you prefer luxury and elegance, a cozy and intimate atmosphere, or a back-to-nature experience, the diverse range of accommodations in the region ensures that you'll find a place to call your home away from home during your visit.

Language and Currency:

Language:

French is the primary language spoken throughout the Loire Valley region. It is the official language of France and is widely used in all aspects of daily life. While visiting popular tourist areas, you will find that English is commonly understood, especially in hotels, restaurants, and attractions catering to international visitors. However, venturing off the beaten path or interacting with locals in smaller towns and villages may require some basic knowledge of French.

Learning a few essential French phrases can greatly enhance your travel experience and help you navigate daily interactions. Polite greetings such as "Bonjour" (Hello), "Merci" (Thank you), and "Au revoir" (Goodbye) are always appreciated and can go a long way in establishing a friendly connection. Additionally, knowing simple phrases like "Parlez-vous anglais?" (Do you speak English?) or "Pouvez-vous m'aider, s'il vous plaît?" (Can you help me, please?) can be useful in seeking assistance when needed.

Currency:

The currency used in France, including the Loire Valley, is the Euro (€). It is recommended to carry some cash for smaller establishments, markets, and rural areas where card payments may be less common. ATMs (automated teller machines), locally known as "Distributeurs Automatiques de Billets" or simply "DAB," are readily available in towns and cities throughout the region. These ATMs accept major credit and debit cards and provide a convenient way to withdraw cash in Euros.

Credit cards are widely accepted in most hotels, restaurants, shops, and tourist attractions in the Loire Valley. Visa and

Mastercard are commonly used, with some establishments also accepting American Express and other major card networks. It is always a good idea to inform your bank or credit card company about your travel plans to avoid any issues with international transactions.

When making purchases or dining out, it is customary to leave a tip in France. Service charges are often included in the bill, but it is common to round up the total or leave a small additional amount as a gesture of appreciation for good service. However, tipping is discretionary, and if you receive exceptional service, you can choose to leave a higher tip accordingly.

In addition to learning some basic French phrases and understanding the local currency, here are a few more tips to help you navigate language and financial matters in the Loire Valley:

Language:

- Phrasebook or Language App: Consider carrying a small phrasebook or installing a language app on your smartphone. These resources can provide you with useful phrases, pronunciation guides, and translations that can come in handy when communicating with locals.
- Politeness and Etiquette: French culture places great importance on politeness and proper etiquette. Using polite phrases such as "s'il vous plaît" (please) and "excusez-moi" (excuse me) can help you create a positive impression and foster a friendly atmosphere during interactions.
- Ask for Assistance: If you find yourself in a situation where language barriers make communication

challenging, don't hesitate to ask for help. Locals are often willing to assist, and many younger people in urban areas have a good command of English.

Currency:

- Cash vs. Cards: While credit cards are widely accepted, it's advisable to carry some cash for small purchases, local markets, or establishments that may not accept cards. Additionally, some rural areas or smaller businesses may have limited card payment facilities. Having a combination of cash and cards will ensure you have payment options in various situations.
- Notify Your Bank: Before you depart for your trip, inform your bank or credit card company about your travel plans. This prevents any unexpected card holds or issues when using your cards abroad. Banks may also provide information on any foreign transaction fees or notify you of any security measures they have in place.
- Currency Exchange: If you need to exchange currency, airports and larger cities have foreign exchange bureaus where you can convert your money. However, these locations may have higher fees or less favorable exchange rates compared to local banks or ATMs. It's recommended to compare rates and fees to get the best value for your money.
- Keep Small Denominations: Having smaller bills and coins on hand can be useful for smaller purchases, tipping, or situations where exact change is needed. It's a good practice to keep a variety of denominations to accommodate different transactions.

- Safety and Security: Just like in any other destination, it's essential to be mindful of your belongings and personal safety. Be cautious when handling cash and avoid openly displaying large sums of money. Use secure ATMs, preferably located within reputable banks or well-lit areas.

By being prepared with basic language skills, understanding the local currency, and following these tips, you can navigate language barriers and financial matters with ease during your visit to the Loire Valley. Embrace the local culture, interact with the friendly locals, and enjoy the unique experiences this captivating region has to offer.

By familiarizing yourself with these practicalities and tips, you will be well-equipped to embark on an unforgettable journey through the Loire Valley, ready to explore its treasures, immerse yourself in its culture, and create lifelong memories.

Chapter 1: Discovering the Châteaux

Château de Chambord: Majestic Grandeur in the Wilderness

History and Architecture

The Château de Chambord, with its remarkable architectural brilliance and grandeur, stands as a captivating testament to the rich history and cultural heritage of the Loire Valley. Construction of this iconic château began in 1519, during the reign of King Francis I, who commissioned its creation as a hunting lodge and a symbol of his power and prestige.

The château's design reflects the artistic influences of the time, blending French Renaissance and classical Italian architectural styles. It was conceived by a team of skilled architects, including Dominique de Cortone and Philibert Delorme, who worked on its construction over several decades. The result is a magnificent structure characterized by its imposing scale, intricate details, and harmonious proportions.

The sheer size of Château de Chambord is awe-inspiring. It boasts 440 rooms, 365 fireplaces, and an astonishing 84 staircases, showcasing the extravagance and opulence of the French monarchy. The most famous feature of the château is its double helix staircase, often attributed to Leonardo da Vinci, which serves as a focal point and a symbol of the architectural prowess of the era. This unique staircase consists of two intertwined spiral ramps that ascend independently without ever meeting, allowing separate access for ascending and descending guests.

Interestingly, despite its grandeur and royal origins, Château de Chambord was rarely used as a residence by the kings of France. Due to its remote location and the monarchs' preference for other palaces, such as the nearby Château de Blois, Chambord was often left vacant. Nevertheless, this lack of extensive occupation contributed to the preservation of its original architectural features and historical integrity.

Throughout its storied history, Château de Chambord experienced various transformations and faced numerous challenges. It witnessed political unrest, including the French Revolution, which led to its nationalization. The château changed hands several times, serving as a symbol of power for different rulers and enduring periods of neglect and disrepair.

Fortunately, in the 19th century, Château de Chambord underwent a significant restoration, initiated by the French government. This restoration effort aimed to preserve its architectural heritage and transform it into a national monument. Today, the château is recognized as a UNESCO World Heritage site and stands as one of the most iconic and visited landmarks in France.

Visitors to Château de Chambord can immerse themselves in its captivating history and explore its magnificent interiors. Walking through the grand salons, royal chambers, and the awe-inspiring double helix staircase, one can't help but be transported back in time to an era of royal splendor. The château's exterior is equally impressive, with its striking façade, towers, and expansive grounds, inviting visitors to wander through its vast parkland and marvel at its beauty.

Beyond its architectural splendor and historical legacy, Château de Chambord holds a special place in the hearts of visitors who are enchanted by its charm and mystique. The château's allure extends beyond its physical attributes, inviting exploration and igniting the imagination.

The surrounding Chambord Park further enhances the allure of the château. Encompassing an expansive area of more than 5,000 hectares, the park offers a serene and picturesque setting. Within its boundaries, visitors can discover enchanting forests, tranquil lakes, and rolling meadows that provide a tranquil escape from the bustling world outside. The park's landscape was intentionally designed to harmonize with the grandeur of the château, showcasing the seamless integration of nature and architecture.

As visitors traverse the park, they may encounter various wildlife species that call this vast wilderness home. Deer, boars, and a variety of bird species can be spotted, offering a glimpse into the biodiversity of the Loire Valley region. The opportunity to witness such natural beauty in close proximity to the château adds an element of enchantment to the overall experience.

Throughout the year, Château de Chambord hosts a range of special events, exhibitions, and cultural performances that enrich the visitor experience. From art exhibitions and concerts to historical reenactments and themed festivals, these events offer a chance to delve deeper into the history, art, and cultural heritage associated with the château. Attending one of these events can provide a unique perspective and a more immersive understanding of the château's significance.

For those seeking a truly immersive and memorable experience, it is worth considering an extended stay in the vicinity of Château de Chambord. Several charming accommodations, including boutique hotels and traditional guesthouses, are located nearby, offering a chance to embrace the tranquility of the Loire Valley and fully immerse oneself in the château's ambiance. Such accommodations often provide a combination of modern comforts and a sense of historical charm, ensuring a delightful and authentic stay.

In addition to exploring the château and its surroundings, visitors can take advantage of the nearby attractions and activities available in the Loire Valley. The region is renowned for its vineyards and wine production, making it an ideal destination for wine enthusiasts to indulge in tastings and tours. Cycling routes, walking trails, and boat trips along the Loire River provide opportunities for outdoor exploration and discovering the natural beauty of the valley.

Whether it's marveling at the architectural marvels of Château de Chambord, immersing oneself in the surrounding parkland, or participating in the vibrant events and activities, a visit to this majestic château is a journey through history, art, and nature. It leaves visitors with a profound appreciation for the cultural heritage of the Loire Valley and a lasting impression of the grandeur and magnificence embodied by Château de Chambord.

Highlights and Must-See Features

Exploring the Château de Chambord is like stepping into a fairytale. The moment you lay eyes on its exterior, you are greeted by a sight that is nothing short of awe-inspiring. The château's architecture is a masterpiece in itself, featuring intricate stone carvings, towering turrets, and an iconic double helix staircase attributed to the genius of Leonardo da Vinci. This double helix staircase is a true marvel of engineering and design, with two spiral staircases that ascend independently, never crossing paths. As you witness this architectural wonder, you can't help but be amazed by the craftsmanship and ingenuity of the artisans who brought it to life.

Once inside the château, a world of opulence and grandeur awaits. Visitors have the opportunity to explore the lavish chambers, grand salons, and royal apartments that were once occupied by French monarchs. Every room is adorned with exquisite tapestries, ornate furniture, and elaborate decorations that offer a glimpse into the extravagant lifestyle of the nobility. The attention to detail is remarkable, and you'll find yourself marveling at the artistry and craftsmanship that went into creating such a lavish living space.

One of the highlights of the Château de Chambord is its rooftop terraces. As you ascend to the top, you are rewarded with panoramic views of the surrounding countryside. The vista stretches as far as the eye can see, encompassing rolling hills, lush forests, and the meandering Loire River. It's a breathtaking sight that allows you to fully appreciate the château's picturesque location and its harmonious integration with the natural landscape.

Beyond the château itself, Chambord Park is a destination of its own. Encompassing over 5,000 hectares, the park is a vast wilderness teeming with diverse flora and fauna. As you explore the park's trails, you'll encounter serene lakes reflecting the château's grandeur, ancient trees standing as silent witnesses to history, and perhaps even catch a glimpse of local wildlife such as deer or rare bird species. The park invites visitors to take leisurely strolls, rent bicycles for a more active adventure, or simply find a picturesque spot for a relaxing picnic. Additionally, horseback riding and boat rides along the Loire River offer additional ways to immerse yourself in the park's natural beauty.

A visit to Château de Chambord and its surrounding park is an experience that combines history, art, and the splendor of nature. It's an opportunity to delve into the enchanting world of French royalty, admire architectural marvels, and reconnect with the serenity of the Loire Valley.

As you explore the vast Chambord Park, you'll find yourself immersed in a realm of natural wonders. The park's sprawling wilderness encompasses a diverse range of ecosystems, making it a haven for nature enthusiasts and outdoor adventurers alike. The park is home to an abundance of flora and fauna, with vibrant meadows, tranquil lakes, and ancient forests that have stood the test of time.

Taking a leisurely stroll along the park's well-maintained trails allows you to fully appreciate the beauty of your surroundings. Each step unveils new discoveries, from delicate wildflowers carpeting the ground to the towering trees that provide shade and a sense of tranquility. The gentle melodies of birdsong fill the air, creating a symphony of nature's own composition.

For those seeking a more active experience, renting a bicycle is a popular choice. Pedaling along the park's designated cycling routes offers a sense of freedom as you navigate through the picturesque landscapes. The winding paths take you on a journey through meadows adorned with colorful blooms, past peaceful ponds where ducks and swans gracefully glide, and alongside the mighty Loire River, which flows majestically through the park.

As you venture deeper into the Chambord Park, keep your eyes peeled for encounters with local wildlife. The park is a habitat for a variety of animals, including deer, wild boars, and an array of bird species. If luck is on your side, you may even spot a fox or witness the graceful flight of a bird of prey. These encounters with nature add an element of wonder and remind you of the interconnectedness of all living things.

For a serene interlude, finding the perfect spot for a picnic is a delightful option. You can spread out a blanket under the shade of a tree, basking in the gentle breeze as you savor a delicious meal surrounded by the park's natural splendor. The peaceful ambiance and idyllic setting create a moment of pure bliss, allowing you to fully appreciate the harmonious coexistence of man-made and natural beauty.

To truly embrace the essence of the Chambord Park, consider embarking on a boat ride along the Loire River. Drifting along the tranquil waters, you'll be treated to breathtaking views of the château's magnificent façade from a different perspective. The rhythmic flow of the river and the captivating reflections on its surface create a sense of serenity and introspection, further enhancing the enchantment of your Chambord experience.

Whether you choose to explore the Château de Chambord's opulent interior, wander through the Chambord Park's untamed landscapes, or immerse yourself in a combination of both, your visit to this iconic destination in the Loire Valley promises to be an extraordinary journey. It is a place where history, architecture, and nature converge, leaving an indelible impression and a lasting connection to the allure of this fairytale-like destination.

Insider Tips for an Enhanced Experience

To make the most of your visit to Château de Chambord, here are some insider tips:

Consider taking a guided tour: While exploring the Château de Chambord on your own is a wonderful experience, joining a guided tour can elevate your visit to another level. Knowledgeable guides are well-versed in the château's history, architecture, and hidden details, and they can provide fascinating insights that you might otherwise miss. They can share captivating stories about the royal residents, the construction process, and the cultural significance of Chambord. They may also reveal lesser-known facts and anecdotes that add depth to your understanding of this architectural masterpiece. A guided tour allows you to appreciate the château from an expert's perspective and gain a comprehensive understanding of its historical and artistic significance.

Visit during weekdays and off-peak hours: Château de Chambord attracts a significant number of visitors, especially during weekends and peak travel seasons. To ensure a more tranquil and immersive experience, it's advisable to plan your visit on weekdays and during off-peak hours. By avoiding the busiest times, you can explore the château at a more relaxed pace and fully soak in its grandeur. Early morning visits offer a serene atmosphere and provide an opportunity to witness the château waking up to the day, while late afternoon visits often allow you to enjoy the golden hour and capture beautiful photographs with fewer people around. This way, you can savor the details and ambiance of the château with a greater sense of tranquility.

Explore the park: The beauty of Château de Chambord extends beyond its magnificent architecture. Don't miss the chance to immerse yourself in the vast Chambord Park that surrounds the château. Renting a bike or taking a leisurely walk through the park allows you to discover its hidden corners, charming bridges, and picturesque landscapes. As you meander along the park's trails, you'll encounter serene lakes reflecting the château's image, ancient trees offering shade and tranquility, and perhaps even stumble upon wildlife like deer or rabbits. The park provides a refreshing escape into nature, offering a perfect complement to the château visit and an opportunity to appreciate the surrounding wilderness that has remained relatively unchanged for centuries.

Attend special events and exhibitions: Château de Chambord frequently hosts special events, exhibitions, and cultural performances that add an extra layer of enchantment to your visit. Stay updated by checking the château's official website or inquiring locally about any upcoming events during your stay. Attending a concert in the château's courtyard, exploring a temporary art exhibition within its walls, or witnessing a historical reenactment can transport you back in time and create unforgettable memories. These events often provide unique access to certain areas of the château or offer a chance to experience Chambord in a different light, adding a touch of magic and exclusivity to your overall visit.

Make a reservation in advance: Due to the popularity of Château de Chambord, it is advisable to make a reservation in advance, especially if you plan to take a guided tour or participate in any special events. Reserving your spot ensures that you can secure a preferred time slot for your visit and guarantees entry even during busy periods. It is recommended to check the château's official website or contact their visitor center to make your reservation and obtain any necessary tickets or passes.

Take your time to appreciate the details: As you explore the Château de Chambord, take your time to soak in the intricate details of the architecture and the rich decorative elements. Pay attention to the ornate ceiling designs, the finely carved stone embellishments, and the intricate woodwork throughout the château. Each room has its own unique features and historical significance, so be sure to observe and appreciate the craftsmanship that went into creating this magnificent structure.

Visit the rooftops for panoramic views: One of the highlights of Château de Chambord is the opportunity to ascend to the rooftop terraces. Climb the stairs or take the elevator to the upper levels and step out onto the terraces for breathtaking panoramic views of the surrounding landscape. From this vantage point, you can admire the sprawling park, the nearby forests, and the winding Loire River. The rooftop views provide a different perspective and allow you to fully appreciate the château's grandeur in its natural setting.

Engage with the interactive exhibits: Château de Chambord has interactive exhibits that offer a hands-on and immersive experience. These exhibits provide an opportunity to learn more about the construction techniques used during the château's creation, the daily life of its inhabitants, and the historical context in which it was built. Interact with the exhibits, watch multimedia presentations, and engage with the informative displays to deepen your understanding of the château's significance in French history and architecture.

Support the preservation efforts: Château de Chambord is a historic treasure that requires ongoing conservation and preservation. Consider supporting the château's efforts by making a donation or purchasing souvenirs from the on-site gift shop. Your contribution helps maintain this cultural landmark for future generations and ensures that its beauty and historical importance can continue to be enjoyed by visitors from around the world.

By following these additional tips, you can make the most of your visit to Château de Chambord, ensuring a memorable and enriching experience. Immerse yourself in the details, take advantage of the various perspectives, engage with the exhibits, and support the preservation efforts to truly appreciate the magnificence and historical significance of this iconic Loire Valley gem.

Château de Chenonceau: A Bridge between Elegance and History

Uncovering the Fascinating Past

The Château de Chenonceau stands not only as a magnificent architectural marvel but also as a place steeped in rich history, captivating visitors with its intriguing past. This iconic château, dating back to the 16th century, holds within its walls a tapestry of stories that have shaped its existence and contributed to its significance in French history.

In exploring the origins of Château de Chenonceau, one is transported back in time to the Renaissance era. Delve into the history of its construction, marveling at the craftsmanship and architectural brilliance that went into creating this masterpiece. Discover the influential figures who played a vital role in its development, such as Diane de Poitiers and Catherine de' Medici. These notable individuals left an indelible mark on the château, leaving their distinct imprints on its design and legacy.

Royal intrigues are interwoven into the very fabric of Château de Chenonceau's history. Uncover the tales of love, jealousy, and political maneuvering that unfolded within its walls. The château became a stage for power struggles among the royal elite, where personal rivalries and dynastic ambitions clashed. These stories shed light on the dramatic events that shaped the course of French history, and Château de Chenonceau stood as a silent witness to it all.

The impact of wars, including the French Revolution, left their mark on Château de Chenonceau. Learn about the challenges faced during times of conflict and upheaval. Discover the resilience and determination of those who sought to preserve the château's architectural integrity and historical significance. Through restoration efforts, the château was brought back to its former glory, allowing visitors to experience the grandeur and beauty that had been temporarily overshadowed by the ravages of war.

The history of Château de Chenonceau is a testament to the enduring spirit of its people and the enduring legacy of this remarkable place. As visitors delve into its past, they are transported to a bygone era, where tales of power, love, and resilience come alive. The château stands today as a living testament to the rich heritage of France and a symbol of the artistry and craftsmanship of the Renaissance period.

The Château de Chenonceau, with its fascinating history, has witnessed the ebb and flow of time, enduring both triumphs and challenges. It has become a testament to the resilience and determination of those who have fought to preserve its architectural splendor and cultural significance.

Throughout its storied past, the château has weathered the storms of war, emerging as a symbol of resilience. The French Revolution brought about a period of upheaval, during which the château faced the threat of destruction. However, thanks to the efforts of dedicated individuals, it was saved from ruin and carefully restored to its former glory. This preservation work not only aimed to safeguard the physical structure but also sought to maintain the historical essence and cultural importance of Château de Chenonceau.

Walking through the halls and rooms of the château, visitors can imagine the events that unfolded within its walls. They can envision the lavish balls and extravagant banquets hosted by the powerful figures of the time. They can sense the whispers of secret meetings and clandestine affairs that occurred behind closed doors. The echoes of history reverberate through the corridors, creating an atmosphere of intrigue and fascination.

Today, Château de Chenonceau stands as a cherished treasure, offering visitors a glimpse into the opulent lifestyle of the past. Its exquisite architecture, characterized by elegant arches and delicate stonework, is a testament to the artistic prowess of the Renaissance period. The château's remarkable location, spanning across the Cher River, adds to its allure, as the iconic arched bridge creates a unique and breathtaking sight.

Exploring the Gardens and Grounds

As you venture beyond the magnificent façade of Château de Chenonceau, you'll find yourself immersed in the enchanting beauty of its gardens and grounds. These meticulously designed landscapes offer a serene and picturesque experience, inviting you to explore and appreciate nature's splendor. Let us take you on a journey through the remarkable gardens and grounds of Château de Chenonceau.

As you stroll through the château's formal gardens, you'll be captivated by the meticulous attention to detail and the timeless elegance they exude. Designed in the classic French Renaissance style, these gardens showcase symmetrical patterns, vibrant flower beds, and carefully sculpted hedges. Every step you take reveals a new vista of harmoniously arranged flora, creating a sense of tranquility and visual delight. Marvel at the precision with which the gardeners have maintained the horticultural masterpiece, ensuring that it remains a true reflection of the château's grandeur.

A delightful feature that awaits you at Château de Chenonceau is the green maze. This playful addition to the grounds provides a delightful experience for visitors of all ages. Enter the maze and let yourself get lost in the winding paths and towering hedges. As you navigate your way through the twists and turns, a sense of whimsy and adventure fills the air. Discover hidden corners, uncover secret passages, and enjoy the thrill of finding your way out. The green maze adds an element of fun and discovery, adding to the overall enchantment of the château's grounds.

One of the highlights of the Château de Chenonceau experience is the opportunity to immerse yourself in the riot of colors that adorn the flower gardens. The meticulously cultivated flower beds showcase a mesmerizing array of blossoms, each boasting its own unique hue and fragrance. As you stroll through these gardens, be prepared to be enchanted by the sights and scents that surround you. Take a moment to admire the delicate petals, breathe in the intoxicating fragrances, and let the beauty of nature envelop your senses. It's a true feast for the eyes and a chance to capture the essence of natural beauty in this idyllic setting.

The gardens and grounds of Château de Chenonceau provide a harmonious extension of the château itself. They offer a respite from the grandeur of the architecture, inviting you to connect with nature and find moments of tranquility. Whether you're marveling at the symmetrical formal gardens, getting delightfully lost in the green maze, or immersing yourself in the vibrant flower gardens, each step reveals a new facet of beauty. Château de Chenonceau's gardens and grounds are a testament to the meticulous craftsmanship and dedication to creating a haven of serenity and visual splendor amidst its historical walls.

The formal gardens of Château de Chenonceau provide a visual feast for visitors. Every aspect of these gardens has been carefully curated to reflect the elegance and grace of the château. As you stroll along the manicured pathways, you'll be mesmerized by the symmetrical layout, where precision and harmony reign supreme. The vibrant flower beds burst with colors, displaying a meticulously planned palette that changes with the seasons. Each blossom seems to vie for your attention, competing in a magnificent display of nature's artistry.

The carefully sculpted hedges that line the pathways add a touch of architectural sophistication to the gardens. Trimmed to perfection, they stand as a testament to the expertise of the gardeners who have maintained these landscapes for generations. As you admire the precision of the hedge work, you'll feel a sense of awe at the level of craftsmanship that has gone into creating these living sculptures. The hedges not only enhance the visual appeal of the gardens but also provide a sense of privacy and intimacy, allowing visitors to lose themselves in the beauty that surrounds them.

As you make your way through the château's grounds, the green maze beckons you to embark on a whimsical adventure. This playful feature adds an element of fun and intrigue to your visit. Step into the maze, and you'll find yourself surrounded by tall hedges that create a sense of mystery and anticipation. As you navigate the winding paths, your excitement grows with each turn, not knowing what lies ahead. This interactive experience allows you to tap into your inner explorer, as you search for the center of the maze or discover hidden surprises along the way. Whether you're traveling with family or seeking a moment of childlike wonder, the green maze offers an enchanting escapade for all.

No visit to Château de Chenonceau's gardens would be complete without immersing yourself in the breathtaking beauty of the flower gardens. Here, you'll find yourself surrounded by a tapestry of colors, where vibrant blooms create a symphony of scents and visual delights. As you walk among the flower beds, you'll witness a captivating display of nature's artistry. Roses, tulips, dahlias, and countless other flowers vie for your attention, each one more exquisite than the last. Take the time to stop and appreciate the intricate details of each blossom, marveling at the delicate petals and the intoxicating fragrances they emit. The flower gardens provide a serene sanctuary, where you can unwind, rejuvenate, and connect with the beauty that surrounds you.

The gardens and grounds of Château de Chenonceau are a testament to the harmonious blend of art and nature. They invite visitors to wander, reflect, and find solace in the serene ambiance they offer. The formal gardens, green maze, and flower gardens create a multisensory experience, allowing you to explore, immerse yourself in nature's beauty, and create lasting memories. As you leave the château's gardens behind, you'll carry with you a sense of tranquility and a renewed appreciation for the timeless allure of this remarkable place.

Unique Experiences and Events

Château de Chenonceau not only offers a glimpse into the past but also provides a myriad of unique experiences and hosts special events that add a touch of magic to your visit. Immerse yourself in the enchantment of this historic landmark and discover the unforgettable moments that await you at Château de Chenonceau.

Wine Tastings:

Indulge your senses in the world-renowned wines produced from the vineyards that surround Château de Chenonceau. As you savor each sip, you'll embark on a delightful journey through the flavors and aromas of the region. Engage in wine tastings led by knowledgeable sommeliers who will share their expertise and guide you through the nuances of the local varietals. Learn about the winemaking traditions that have been passed down through generations, gaining a deeper appreciation for the artistry behind each bottle. Whether you're a wine connoisseur or simply enjoy a good glass of wine, this experience will create unforgettable memories for your palate.

Concerts and Cultural Events:

Immerse yourself in the ambiance of Château de Chenonceau through its enchanting concerts and cultural events. Step into the château's historical setting and be transported to a time when music and arts flourished. Experience live music performances that resonate through the grand halls, filling them with melodies that evoke emotions and capture the spirit of the past. From classical concerts to contemporary performances, the château becomes a stage for talent and creativity. Additionally, theater productions and exhibitions breathe life into the historical backdrop, bringing stories and artistic expressions to life. These cultural events create a captivating atmosphere, allowing you to engage with the château on a deeper level and immerse yourself in the world of art and entertainment.

Nighttime Illuminations:

Witness the château in a whole new light during the nighttime illuminations. As the sun sets and darkness descends, Château de Chenonceau transforms into a mesmerizing spectacle. Dramatic lighting bathes the architectural details in a soft glow, casting shadows that accentuate the intricate craftsmanship and magnificence of the structure. The illuminated gardens and grounds create a dreamlike ambiance, with the play of light and shadows enhancing the natural beauty of the surroundings. The nighttime illuminations evoke a sense of romance and wonder, as you stroll through the château's corridors and gardens, discovering hidden corners illuminated with an ethereal glow. This magical experience allows you to see Château de Chenonceau in a whole new dimension, creating lasting memories of its enchanting allure.

Château de Chenonceau beckons you to embrace its history and elegance, but it also invites you to immerse yourself in a world of unique experiences and special events. From the indulgence of wine tastings to the captivating concerts and cultural events, and the breathtaking nighttime illuminations, your visit to Château de Chenonceau will be an extraordinary journey filled with enchantment and wonder.

In addition to wine tastings, concerts, and nighttime illuminations, Château de Chenonceau offers a range of other special experiences and events that will further enhance your visit. Let's explore some of these remarkable offerings:

Gourmet Dining:

Immerse yourself in a culinary journey fit for royalty with gourmet dining experiences at Château de Chenonceau. Indulge in exquisite meals prepared by talented chefs who showcase the finest local ingredients and flavors. Whether it's a romantic candlelit dinner in a historical chamber or a lavish feast in the château's grand hall, each bite will transport you to a world of gastronomic delight, perfectly complementing your exploration of the château's elegance and history.

Art Exhibitions:

Experience the merging of art and history through captivating art exhibitions hosted within the walls of Château de Chenonceau. Discover carefully curated displays featuring renowned artists, both contemporary and classic, whose works reflect the château's spirit and resonate with its architectural grandeur. Immerse yourself in the beauty and creativity of these art exhibitions, which provide a unique perspective on the intersection of art and heritage.

Gardening Workshops:

Tap into your green thumb and join gardening workshops offered at Château de Chenonceau. Learn from expert gardeners who will guide you through the techniques and principles behind the château's immaculate gardens. Gain hands-on experience in planting, pruning, and maintaining various types of flora, all while immersed in the picturesque surroundings. These workshops offer a chance to connect with the château's horticultural legacy and provide practical knowledge that you can apply to your own gardening endeavors.

Historical Reenactments:

Transport yourself back in time through engaging historical reenactments that bring the past to life. Witness costumed actors portraying key figures and events from the château's history, recreating scenes that shed light on its significance and cultural context. Whether it's a royal procession, a lively market scene, or a dramatic reenactment of historical milestones, these performances provide a captivating window into the past and offer a unique way to engage with the château's heritage.

Guided Tours:

Take advantage of guided tours led by knowledgeable experts who will unveil the château's secrets and provide deeper insights into its historical and architectural significance. Accompanied by a professional guide, you'll have the opportunity to explore hidden chambers, uncover lesser-known stories, and appreciate the fine details and craftsmanship that make Château de Chenonceau a true masterpiece. These guided tours offer a rich and immersive experience, allowing you to fully appreciate the château's cultural and historical importance.

Château de Chenonceau is not just a static monument frozen in time; it is a living testament to the past, continuously offering new and enchanting experiences. Whether you choose to indulge in gourmet dining, immerse yourself in art, participate in gardening workshops, witness historical reenactments, or join guided tours, each experience will deepen your connection with the château, creating cherished memories that will stay with you long after your visit.

Château de Chenonceau is a place where elegance and history merge seamlessly. By exploring its fascinating past, strolling through its beautiful gardens, and immersing yourself in unique experiences and events, you will truly appreciate the magic and allure of this iconic château.

Château de Blois: A Royal Residence with a Story to Tell

Royal History and Intriguing Anecdotes

The Château de Blois stands proudly as a testament to the rich tapestry of history that has unfolded in the Loire Valley. As you step into its grand halls and elegant chambers, you are transported back in time, immersing yourself in the royal heritage that has shaped this magnificent residence. From its construction in the 13th century to its status as a favored dwelling of French kings, the château has been a silent witness to pivotal moments that have shaped the course of history.

As you wander through the château's corridors, you'll discover a treasure trove of captivating anecdotes that bring the past to life. One such remarkable inhabitant is Queen Catherine de' Medici, a figure both revered and feared. During the tumultuous period of the French Wars of

Religion, Catherine utilized the château as her power base, making it a center of political intrigue and power struggles. Unravel the tales of her influence, ambition, and the web of alliances and rivalries that defined her reign.

Beyond the stories of Catherine de' Medici, the château holds countless other captivating narratives. Immerse yourself in the dramatic tales of royal love affairs, scandals, and personal triumphs that played out within its walls. Each room conceals secrets waiting to be discovered, each corridor whispers tales of passion, betrayal, and the pursuit of power. The Château de Blois has been witness to the rise and fall of dynasties, the clash of ideologies, and the resilience of the human spirit.

Step into the Royal Apartments and envision the opulent lifestyle of French royalty. Admire the grandeur of the King's Chambers and imagine the power and authority that emanated from this very place. Move through the Queen's Apartments and let the whispers of historical figures guide you through their triumphs and tribulations. Stand at the center of the château's courtyard and feel the echoes of history reverberating through the stone walls.

Every visit to the Château de Blois is an opportunity to delve into the captivating narratives that have shaped its legacy. As you explore its rooms, corridors, and hidden corners, you become a part of its history, a participant in the stories that unfolded within its embrace. The château's royal heritage and the intriguing anecdotes of its inhabitants transport you to a bygone era, where the dramas of courtly life unfolded with all its complexities and splendor.

Immersing yourself in the captivating narratives of the Château de Blois, you begin to grasp the immense historical significance of this grand residence. The château's walls have seen monarchs rise and fall, witnessed treaties forged and battles waged, and served as a backdrop to the ebb and flow of power.

As you explore the château's chambers, imagine the whispers of the past echoing through the corridors. Picture the lavish banquets held in the Great Hall, where kings and queens entertained foreign dignitaries and nobles from near and far. Feel the weight of the decisions made in the Council Room, where political alliances were forged and fates were sealed.

The château's architecture itself tells a story. From its medieval beginnings, evident in the fortified towers and defensive features, to the Renaissance additions that brought elegance and refinement, the evolution of the château reflects the changing tastes and aspirations of its occupants. Marvel at the intricate stonework, the delicate carvings, and the graceful arches that adorn its façade. Each architectural detail carries a historical significance, a testament to the artistic achievements of its time.

Venturing into the inner chambers, you encounter rooms steeped in history and intrigue. Stand in the Queen's Bedchamber, where Catherine de' Medici resided and made critical decisions that shaped the destiny of France. As you explore the King's Study, visualize the kings engrossed in matters of state, contemplating the welfare of their kingdom.

The Château de Blois also houses a remarkable collection of art and artifacts that further enrich the visitor's experience. Admire the tapestries that line the walls, depicting scenes from mythology and history. Marvel at the masterful portraits that capture the likeness and personality of past rulers and their entourage. Each artwork offers a glimpse into the artistic achievements of the time and provides a deeper understanding of the château's cultural significance.

To fully appreciate your visit to the Château de Blois, take advantage of the practical information and visitor's guide provided. Plan your visit to coincide with guided tours led by knowledgeable experts who can shed light on the historical context and significance of each room and artwork. Make note of the opening hours and any special events or exhibitions taking place during your visit.

As you depart the château, you carry with you not only memories of its grandeur but also a sense of connection to the rich heritage of the Loire Valley. The Château de Blois stands as a testament to the enduring allure of history, inviting visitors to step into the past and become part of its extraordinary narrative.

Architectural Marvels and Notable Artworks

The Château de Blois is a true architectural gem that leaves visitors in awe with its remarkable fusion of various styles spanning across the centuries. From its medieval origins to its Renaissance and classical additions, the château stands as a testament to the evolving tastes and influences that have shaped its unique character.

As you approach the château, your eyes will be drawn to the intricate details of its Gothic façade. Adorned with delicate sculptures and ornate tracery, the façade showcases the craftsmanship and attention to detail characteristic of the Gothic architectural style. Each intricate carving and architectural feature tells a story of the past, transporting you back to a time of knights, castles, and medieval grandeur.

Upon stepping inside, you'll be greeted by the stunning Renaissance wing of the château. This section of the residence showcases the opulence and refinement of the Renaissance era. The Francis I Gallery, a highlight of the Renaissance wing, is a true masterpiece. Adorned with intricate frescoes depicting scenes of courtly life, this gallery provides a window into the rich history and artistic achievements of the period. As you walk through the gallery, you'll be immersed in a world of elegance and splendor, surrounded by the works of talented artists who left their mark on this royal residence.

Exploring the different wings and apartments of the château, you'll encounter remarkable examples of architectural innovation and artistic expression. From grand halls with towering ceilings to intimate chambers adorned with rich tapestries and ornate furnishings, each space tells its own story and reflects the changing tastes and aspirations of the château's inhabitants throughout history. The architectural details, such as intricately carved fireplaces, soaring staircases, and beautifully crafted ceilings, are testaments to the skill and vision of the craftsmen who contributed to the château's construction and renovation over the centuries.

Beyond its architectural wonders, the Château de Blois is also home to a remarkable collection of artwork. As you explore the rooms and corridors, you'll encounter magnificent masterpieces that have been carefully preserved and displayed within the château's walls. From exquisite tapestries that depict grand scenes to majestic portraits of royal figures, the artwork offers a glimpse into the artistic achievements of the past. Each piece tells its own story, revealing insights into the lives and aspirations of those who once called this château home.

Marvel at the richly woven tapestries, where intricate details and vibrant colors come together to create stunning visual narratives. Admire the brushstrokes and techniques employed by renowned artists, capturing the essence of the era and the individuals portrayed. The château's collection of artwork is a treasure trove of cultural and historical significance, providing visitors with a deeper appreciation for the artistic achievements of the past.

Each visit to the Château de Blois is a journey through time, where the walls whisper stories of kings, queens, and the courtly life that once filled its halls. As you wander through the different wings and apartments, you'll come across rooms that have been meticulously preserved to reflect their original splendor.

One such room is the Royal Apartments, where you can witness the lavish lifestyle of the French monarchy. Adorned with rich tapestries, gilded ceilings, and finely carved furniture, these chambers immerse you in the opulence of the past. Imagine the grandeur of banquets and balls held within these walls as you take in the intricate details and decorative elements.

As you continue your exploration, don't miss the exquisite Chapel of St. Calais, a hidden gem within the château. This small chapel showcases intricate stained glass windows that filter colorful rays of light into the space. It's a serene and sacred place that invites reflection and offers a glimpse into the religious practices of the time.

The château's architectural wonders extend beyond its interior. Venture out into the beautifully landscaped gardens, where meticulously manicured lawns, fragrant flower beds, and elegant fountains create a picturesque setting. Take a leisurely stroll through the gardens, allowing the tranquility to wash over you as you appreciate the harmonious integration of nature and architecture.

To enhance your understanding of the château's history and significance, consider joining a guided tour. Knowledgeable guides provide in-depth commentary, sharing captivating anecdotes and historical insights that bring the château to life. They will lead you through the various sections, providing context and helping you uncover hidden details that may go unnoticed without their expertise.

Before planning your visit, be sure to check the château's website or contact the visitor's center for the most up-to-date information regarding opening hours, ticket prices, and any special exhibitions or events taking place during your visit. It's also advisable to book your tickets in advance, especially during peak tourist seasons, to ensure a smooth entry and avoid any potential queues.

A visit to the Château de Blois is an immersive experience that transports you to a bygone era of royal splendor, architectural brilliance, and artistic mastery. Take your time to appreciate the intricate details, the captivating stories, and the remarkable collection of artwork that make this château an unmissable destination in the Loire Valley.

Practical Information and Visitor's Guide

To make the most of your visit to the Château de Blois, it's essential to be equipped with practical information and a comprehensive visitor's guide. Here are some key details to help you plan your visit:

Opening Hours:

The opening hours of the Château de Blois may vary, so it's advisable to check the château's official website or consult local tourist information for the most up-to-date information. It's important to note that the château may have different operating hours during certain seasons or holidays. By verifying the opening hours in advance, you can plan your visit accordingly and ensure that you have ample time to explore the château and its many treasures.

Guided Tours:

Consider joining a guided tour when visiting the Château de Blois to gain deeper insights into its rich history and architectural splendor. Knowledgeable guides, well-versed in the château's stories, will provide fascinating commentary as they lead you through the various rooms and chambers. They will highlight the most significant areas of the residence, sharing anecdotes and historical context that will enhance your understanding and appreciation of the château. A guided tour can truly bring the château to life, allowing you to immerse yourself in its captivating past.

Highlights:

When exploring the Château de Blois, there are certain highlights that should not be missed. The Francis I Gallery is an absolute must-see, showcasing intricate frescoes that depict scenes of courtly life and exemplify the artistic achievements of the Renaissance period. The Royal Apartments, where kings and queens once resided, offer a glimpse into their opulent lifestyles and provide a sense of the château's grandeur. Additionally, make sure to visit the château's terrace, as it offers stunning panoramic views of the surrounding landscape. Plan your route accordingly to ensure you have enough time to fully appreciate these captivating features.

Visitor Facilities:

The Château de Blois provides various visitor facilities to enhance your overall experience. Restrooms are conveniently available throughout the château, ensuring your comfort during your visit. Take some time to browse the gift shop, where you can find unique souvenirs and mementos related to the château and its history. If you need a break or a refreshment, the château also has a café where you can relax and indulge in some local delights. These visitor facilities are designed to cater to your needs and ensure a pleasant and enjoyable visit.

Accessibility:

The Château de Blois strives to provide accessibility for all visitors. If you have specific accessibility requirements, it is advisable to check the château's official website or contact them directly for detailed information. They can provide insights into wheelchair accessibility, the availability of ramps or elevators, and any other accommodations that may be necessary to ensure a comfortable visit. The château aims to create an inclusive environment where everyone can appreciate its historical and architectural wonders.

Photography and Filming:

Before taking photographs or filming inside the Château de Blois, it's important to find out about any restrictions or guidelines in place. Some areas of the château may have restrictions to protect delicate artifacts or maintain the historical integrity of the residence. Respect the guidelines and restrictions regarding photography and filming to ensure the preservation of the château and its treasures for future generations to enjoy. Remember, capturing memories is still possible within the designated areas, and photography policies are typically in place to strike a balance between visitor experience and conservation.

By following the guidelines and respecting the photography and filming policies, you can help preserve the historical integrity of the Château de Blois while still capturing cherished memories of your visit. Remember that while photography can be a wonderful way to document your experience, it's equally important to take moments to simply immerse yourself in the ambiance and beauty of the château without the lens.

As you explore the château, take the time to absorb its intricate details, admire the artistic masterpieces, and imagine the stories that unfolded within its walls. Let the captivating atmosphere transport you back in time to the era of kings and queens, and appreciate the preservation efforts that have made it possible to enjoy the château's splendor today.

Before concluding your visit, consider taking a leisurely stroll around the château's exterior. Admire its imposing architecture from different angles and take in the surrounding landscape. The panoramic views from the terrace are particularly breathtaking, offering a picturesque vista of the city and the Loire River.

As you exit the château, take a moment to reflect on the rich history, the fascinating anecdotes, and the architectural marvels that you have encountered. The Château de Blois is not just a royal residence; it's a living testament to the past and an embodiment of the cultural heritage of the Loire Valley. Allow your visit to leave a lasting impression and inspire a continued appreciation for the region's historical treasures.

With practical information, a comprehensive visitor's guide, and a respectful approach to preserving the château's legacy, your experience at the Château de Blois is sure to be memorable. Whether you're a history enthusiast, an architecture lover, or simply someone seeking to immerse themselves in the grandeur of the past, the château offers a captivating journey through time. Embrace the opportunity to explore this royal residence and let its stories unfold before your eyes.

Immerse yourself in the royal history, architectural wonders, and artistic treasures of the Château de Blois. With the practical information and visitor's guide at hand, you'll be ready to embark on an unforgettable journey through the captivating stories and opulence of this remarkable royal residence.

Chapter 2: Immersing in Local Traditions

Gastronomy: A Journey of Flavors

The Loire Valley is renowned for its delectable cuisine, offering a culinary experience that is sure to delight food enthusiasts. In this chapter, we will dive into the gastronomic treasures of the region, exploring savory delights, culinary delicacies, iconic Loire Valley wines, vineyards, and charming cafés and restaurants.

Savory Delights and Culinary Delicacies

Indulge your taste buds in a gastronomic adventure through the Loire Valley's savory delights and culinary delicacies. The region's cuisine is a celebration of its bountiful natural resources, featuring a harmonious blend of traditional dishes and innovative creations that showcase the abundance of fresh local produce and the area's rich agricultural heritage.

One of the highlights of the Loire Valley's gastronomy is its exquisite goat cheese. Renowned for its distinctive flavors and creamy textures, Loire Valley goat cheese is a true delight for cheese connoisseurs. Whether you prefer the mild and delicate Crottin de Chavignol or the robust and pungent Valençay, each bite will transport you to a world of artisanal craftsmanship and unparalleled taste.

Another culinary treasure of the region is the renowned rillettes. These savory spreads are made by slow-cooking shredded pork or duck, seasoned with a blend of aromatic herbs and spices. The result is a melt-in-your-mouth delicacy that perfectly balances rich flavors and tender textures. Spread rillettes on freshly baked baguette slices or pair them with a glass of local wine for a truly indulgent experience.

The Loire Valley's culinary heritage is also deeply rooted in the art of charcuterie. Delve into the world of cured meats, terrines, and pâtés, where local artisans showcase their expertise and passion for preserving meat. Sample the velvety textures of a perfectly cured saucisson, relish the flavors of a decadent pork terrine, or savor the earthy richness of a duck pâté. Accompanied by a glass of wine from the region, these charcuterie delights offer a symphony of flavors that will leave you craving for more.

As you explore the gastronomic landscape of the Loire Valley, be sure not to miss out on trying the famous fouées. These small doughy bread pockets, similar to pita bread, are baked to perfection and served with a variety of fillings. From savory options like rillettes, cheese, or local charcuterie to sweet combinations with honey or jam, fouées provide a unique culinary experience that showcases the region's creativity and versatility.

In addition to the aforementioned culinary delights, the Loire Valley is also known for its abundance of fresh local produce, which plays a significant role in the region's gastronomic scene. As you explore the local markets and farm stands, you'll be greeted by a vibrant array of seasonal fruits and vegetables, aromatic herbs, and fragrant flowers. The fertile lands of the Loire Valley contribute to the cultivation of a diverse range of ingredients, ensuring that the dishes you encounter are bursting with flavor and freshness.

One of the joys of dining in the Loire Valley is the opportunity to experience traditional dishes prepared with a modern twist. Talented chefs infuse classic recipes with their own creative flair, offering a contemporary take on age-old favorites. From innovative interpretations of regional specialties to fusion dishes that blend local and international flavors, the Loire Valley's culinary landscape embraces innovation while honoring its roots.

For those seeking a deeper understanding of the region's gastronomy, culinary workshops and cooking classes are available, allowing you to learn from skilled chefs and artisans. Discover the secrets behind traditional Loire Valley recipes, master the techniques used to create exquisite dishes, and gain insights into the local ingredients and culinary traditions. Whether you're a novice cook or an experienced culinary enthusiast, these immersive experiences provide an opportunity to not only savor the flavors of the Loire Valley but also to bring them back home and recreate the magic in your own kitchen.

To complement the gastronomic journey, the Loire Valley boasts an impressive selection of local wines. The region's vineyards produce a wide range of varietals, from crisp whites to full-bodied reds and elegant rosés. Take the time to visit the vineyards, where you can stroll through the picturesque landscapes, learn about the winemaking process, and, of course, indulge in tastings. Engage with passionate winemakers who will guide you through the characteristics and nuances of their wines, sharing stories and insights that deepen your appreciation for the craftsmanship and dedication behind each bottle.

In the Loire Valley, dining is not just about the food—it's an experience that encompasses the heritage, culture, and passion of the region. From farm-to-table freshness to innovative culinary creations, the Loire Valley's gastronomy invites you to embark on a journey of flavors, where every meal is a celebration of the region's abundant resources and the artistry of its talented chefs and producers. Prepare to indulge your taste buds, expand your culinary horizons, and create memories that will linger long after your visit to this enchanting part of France.

Iconic Loire Valley Wines and Vineyards

The Loire Valley is truly a paradise for wine lovers, earning its reputation as the "Garden of France" due to its extraordinary vineyards and exceptional wines. Prepare to embark on an enchanting journey through the vine-clad hills, where every sip tells a story of craftsmanship and terroir.

One of the highlights of Loire Valley wine is its remarkable variety of white wines. Start your exploration with Muscadet, a crisp and refreshing white wine renowned for its vibrant acidity and minerality. Produced near the Atlantic coast, Muscadet beautifully complements seafood dishes and is best enjoyed chilled on a sunny terrace overlooking the Loire River.

Continue your discovery with the elegant Sauvignon Blancs of Sancerre and Pouilly-Fumé. These wines captivate with their aromatic profiles, featuring notes of citrus, gooseberry, and herbs. Sancerre is known for its vibrant acidity and flinty minerality, while Pouilly-Fumé exhibits a smoky character that adds depth to its aromatic expression. Pair these wines with goat cheese, fresh salads, or grilled fish to fully experience their flavors.

For a truly indulgent experience, venture into the world of Chenin Blancs from Vouvray and Anjou. These luscious wines present a wide range of styles, from dry to sweet, each offering its own unique charm. Discover dry Chenin Blancs with their honeyed aromas, vibrant acidity, and delightful fruit character. Explore demi-sec and moelleux wines, where the natural sweetness of Chenin Blanc grapes is balanced by a refreshing acidity, creating harmonious dessert wines that pair well with foie gras, cheeses, or fruit-based desserts.

As you delve into the Loire Valley's red wines, prepare to be captivated by their depth and elegance. Chinon, Bourgueil, and Saumur are renowned for their red wines crafted primarily from the Cabernet Franc grape variety. Chinon wines impress with their medium-bodied structure, exhibiting red fruit flavors, subtle herbaceous notes, and refined tannins. Bourgueil wines often showcase a touch more richness, with black fruit characteristics, earthy undertones, and supple textures. Saumur reds combine Cabernet Franc with Cabernet Sauvignon, resulting in wines with intense dark fruit flavors, velvety tannins, and a distinct herbal complexity.

To truly appreciate the artistry behind Loire Valley wines, visiting family-owned wineries is a must. Step into the vineyards, where the vines bask in the warm sun and thrive in the region's diverse terroir. Engage with passionate winemakers who are eager to share their knowledge and love for their craft. Learn about the meticulous winemaking process, from vine to bottle, and gain a deeper understanding of the unique characteristics that define each wine. End your winery visits with tastings, allowing your palate to discern the subtle nuances of each vintage. Savor the interplay of flavors, aromas, and textures, and perhaps you'll discover a new favorite wine to bring back home as a treasured memento of your Loire Valley journey.

In addition to visiting wineries, the Loire Valley offers a myriad of wine-related experiences that further enrich your journey through its vine-clad hills.

Immerse yourself in the breathtaking landscapes of the Loire Valley as you embark on scenic wine trails. Explore the vineyards on foot or by bicycle, following designated routes that wind through picturesque villages, rolling hills, and idyllic riverside paths. Marvel at the lush green vineyards stretching as far as the eye can see, and pause to take in the fragrant scents of blooming flowers and earthy vines. The trails offer not only a chance to enjoy the region's natural beauty but also an opportunity to encounter hidden wineries and tasting rooms tucked away in charming countryside settings.

To deepen your understanding of Loire Valley wines, consider attending wine festivals and events that celebrate the region's vinicultural heritage. Experience the lively atmosphere as winemakers and wine enthusiasts come together to share their passion. From small-scale village celebrations to grand-scale events, these gatherings showcase the diversity of Loire Valley wines and offer the chance to taste a wide range of vintages. Participate in wine workshops and seminars led by experts, where you can refine your tasting skills and gain insights into the unique characteristics of different appellations and grape varieties.

Indulge in culinary experiences that perfectly complement the Loire Valley's exceptional wines. Many wineries offer food and wine pairing experiences, where local delicacies are expertly matched with the region's wines to create a symphony of flavors. Delight in a gourmet meal at a vineyard restaurant, where the chef's creations are thoughtfully crafted to enhance the nuances of the wines being served.

Alternatively, join cooking classes that focus on the use of local ingredients and techniques, allowing you to discover firsthand the culinary traditions of the region.

For those seeking a truly immersive wine adventure, consider planning your visit around the annual grape harvest. Participate in the time-honored tradition of picking grapes and experience the excitement and energy that fills the air during this bustling period. Join in the festivities as wineries organize grape-stomping events, where you can roll up your pants and step into a wooden vat filled with grapes, reveling in the tactile experience of crushing the fruit underfoot. This hands-on encounter with winemaking traditions offers a unique perspective and a memorable connection to the process that brings Loire Valley wines to life.

Whether you're a seasoned wine connoisseur or an enthusiastic novice, the Loire Valley beckons with its diverse vineyards, exceptional wines, and immersive wine experiences. Prepare to be captivated by the beauty of the region, the passion of its winemakers, and the sheer pleasure of indulging in world-class wines amidst the enchanting ambiance of the "Garden of France."

Charming Cafés and Restaurants

The Loire Valley's charming cafés and restaurants not only tantalize the taste buds with their delectable meals but also provide an opportunity to immerse oneself in the region's relaxed and inviting ambiance. Start your day on a delightful note by enjoying a leisurely breakfast at a quaint café. Picture yourself seated at a cozy table, basking in the warm sunlight that filters through the café's windows. Indulge in freshly baked croissants, their buttery layers melting in your mouth, accompanied by pain au chocolat, a delectable pastry filled with rich, gooey chocolate. Savor the aroma of a freshly brewed cup of coffee, whether it's a smooth café au lait or a strong espresso, awakening your senses and preparing you for the day ahead.

As lunchtime approaches, the Loire Valley's bistros beckon with their enticing menus. These charming eateries offer a fusion of classic French dishes with a regional twist. Delight in the flavors of Coq au Vin, a hearty dish of chicken braised in red wine with mushrooms and onions, showcasing the region's culinary heritage. Sample the famous Tarte Tatin, a caramelized upside-down apple tart that originated in the Loire Valley, where every bite is a perfect balance of sweetness and buttery pastry. In these bistros, talented chefs expertly prepare and present dishes that highlight the local ingredients, providing a unique and flavorful experience that truly captures the essence of the region.

For a truly enchanting dining experience, the Loire Valley boasts Michelin-starred restaurants that are sure to leave a lasting impression. Indulge in a romantic dinner, where the combination of exceptional cuisine and an elegant setting creates an atmosphere of pure enchantment. These renowned establishments attract culinary talent from around the world, as their chefs showcase their creativity and expertise. Each dish is a work of art, meticulously crafted using locally sourced ingredients that reflect the region's bountiful produce. Allow your taste buds to be taken on a journey of flavors, as you savor every bite of the culinary masterpieces presented before you.

The Loire Valley offers not only delectable meals but also the opportunity to dine alfresco in picturesque towns along the meandering river. Imagine sitting at a table on a sun-drenched terrace, overlooking the tranquil waters of the

Loire. As you savor your meal, the gentle breeze carries the soothing sounds of the river and the rustling of leaves from nearby trees. Accompanied by a glass of fine Loire Valley wine, each sip a harmonious complement to your meal, you can truly appreciate the idyllic setting that surrounds you.

In addition to the diverse range of dining experiences, the Loire Valley also presents a variety of culinary events and festivals throughout the year. These events celebrate the region's gastronomic heritage and provide an opportunity for visitors to engage with local traditions. From food fairs and farmers' markets to wine tastings and cooking demonstrations, there are numerous opportunities to immerse yourself in the vibrant culinary culture of the Loire Valley.

One such event is the annual "Fête de la Gastronomie," a celebration of French cuisine that takes place in September. During this gastronomic extravaganza, the Loire Valley comes alive with food stalls, outdoor feasts, and culinary workshops, allowing you to sample a wide array of dishes and delicacies. From traditional recipes passed down through generations to innovative creations by up-and-coming chefs, the Fête de la Gastronomie showcases the region's culinary creativity and abundance.

For wine enthusiasts, the Loire Valley's vineyards host numerous wine-related events and festivals. The "Vendanges," or grape harvest, is a particularly exciting time to visit. Join in the festivities as locals and visitors come together to pick grapes and celebrate the culmination of a year's hard work in the vineyards. Participate in grape-stomping competitions, enjoy wine tastings, and witness the traditional winemaking process firsthand.

As you explore the charming towns and villages of the Loire Valley, you'll also come across quaint tea rooms and patisseries offering an assortment of delectable pastries, cakes, and macarons. Take a break from sightseeing and indulge in a sweet treat accompanied by a cup of aromatic tea or a frothy cappuccino. These delightful establishments provide a cozy and inviting atmosphere, inviting you to relax and indulge in a moment of culinary bliss.

No visit to the Loire Valley would be complete without experiencing the region's legendary "Table d'Hôtes." In this tradition, local families open their homes and offer guests a chance to dine with them, sharing a home-cooked meal and engaging in lively conversations. This intimate and personal experience provides a glimpse into the everyday lives of the locals while savoring authentic homemade dishes prepared with love and care.

Whether you're a food lover, wine enthusiast, or simply seeking a taste of authentic French cuisine, the Loire Valley's gastronomic offerings are sure to captivate your palate and leave you with a deep appreciation for the region's culinary traditions. From charming cafés and restaurants to culinary events and traditional dining experiences, the Loire Valley presents a feast for the senses, inviting you to indulge in its flavors, aromas, and warm hospitality.

Immerse yourself in the culinary wonders of the Loire Valley, where savory delights, iconic wines, and charming cafés and restaurants converge to create an unforgettable gastronomic experience. Prepare to embark on a flavorsome journey that will leave you with a deep appreciation for the region's culinary traditions and an abundance of cherished food memories.

Traditional Festivals and Events

The Loire Valley is not only known for its magnificent châteaux and picturesque landscapes but also for its vibrant traditional festivals and events that celebrate the rich heritage of the region. Immerse yourself in the cultural tapestry of the Loire Valley by participating in these lively festivities, gaining insight into local customs and folklore, and enjoying unique experiences that will create lasting memories.

Festivities Celebrating Loire Valley Heritage

The Loire Valley's festivals are a gateway to the region's captivating history, allowing visitors to step back in time and experience the grandeur of bygone eras. These vibrant celebrations bring the past to life through grand processions, medieval reenactments, and immersive experiences that transport participants to a different time.

One of the most awe-inspiring festivals in the Loire Valley is the Fête de Jeanne d'Arc in Orléans. This remarkable event commemorates the heroic figure of Joan of Arc, who played a crucial role in the city's history. The festival takes place annually and draws both locals and visitors from around the world. The streets of Orléans come alive with parades featuring elaborately costumed participants, beautifully decorated floats, and marching bands. Historical pageants reenact significant moments from Joan of Arc's life, capturing the spirit of her bravery and determination. The festival also includes concerts showcasing traditional music, theatrical performances, and culinary delights that evoke the atmosphere of the Middle Ages. Through this festival, participants gain a profound appreciation for the historical significance of Orléans and its beloved heroine.

Another enchanting festival in the Loire Valley is the Renaissance Festival in Loches. Set against the backdrop of the town's medieval architecture, this event transports visitors to the splendor of the 16th century. The streets come alive with a vibrant array of characters dressed in period costumes, including nobles, jesters, knights, and damsels. Musicians fill the air with melodies from the Renaissance era, and jugglers and street performers entertain the crowds with their mesmerizing acts. The festival offers an immersive experience as visitors can interact with the costumed characters, learn traditional dances, and witness demonstrations of ancient crafts. Throughout the festival, various exhibitions and shows provide insight into the art, architecture, and culture of the Renaissance period. This event allows visitors to indulge in the magic of the past, appreciating the beauty and cultural richness of the Loire Valley during the Renaissance.

Each festival in the Loire Valley provides a unique opportunity to witness the living history of the region. Whether it's the grandeur of Joan of Arc's commemoration or the splendor of the Renaissance, these festivals bring together locals, historians, and enthusiasts to celebrate and showcase the historical heritage that defines the Loire Valley. The attention to detail in the costumes, the immersive settings, and the carefully curated performances create an atmosphere that transports visitors back in time. By participating in these festivals, visitors not only gain knowledge and appreciation for the region's history but also create cherished memories of being part of the vibrant tapestry of the Loire Valley's past.

As participants immerse themselves in the historical festivals of the Loire Valley, they are surrounded by a vivid re-creation of the past. The attention to detail in the costumes, props, and settings helps create an authentic atmosphere that truly transports visitors to another era. The sight of noble knights on horseback, the sounds of medieval music echoing through the streets, and the aroma of traditional delicacies being prepared all combine to create an unforgettable experience.

During these festivals, historical accuracy is paramount. Expert historians and dedicated enthusiasts work tirelessly to ensure that every aspect of the event reflects the specific time period being celebrated. From the intricately designed costumes based on meticulous research to the faithful reproduction of ancient rituals and traditions, these festivals strive to provide an accurate and educational representation of the region's history.

Beyond the visual and auditory spectacle, the festivals also offer a chance to engage with the past on a personal level. Visitors can participate in interactive workshops where they can learn ancient crafts such as blacksmithing, calligraphy, or traditional dances. This hands-on approach allows individuals to not only observe history but also actively engage with it, gaining a deeper understanding of the skills, techniques, and customs that were prevalent during the era being depicted.

Furthermore, these festivals foster a sense of community and cultural pride among the locals. They serve as a reminder of the region's rich heritage and offer an opportunity for people to come together, celebrate their shared history, and pass down traditions to younger generations. The festivals often involve local artisans, craftsmen, and performers, supporting and promoting the preservation of traditional skills and cultural practices.

For visitors, these festivals provide an extraordinary way to connect with the history of the Loire Valley. The immersive nature of the events allows for a profound appreciation of the region's past, enabling participants to gain insights into the daily lives, customs, and beliefs of those who came before. It is an experience that goes beyond mere observation, offering a deeper connection to the cultural identity and legacy of the Loire Valley.

In conclusion, the historical festivals of the Loire Valley offer an enchanting journey into the region's past. Through grand processions, medieval reenactments, and interactive experiences, visitors are transported to different eras, witnessing the living history of this remarkable region. These festivals serve as a testament to the cultural richness and enduring heritage of the Loire Valley, creating lasting memories and a profound appreciation for its historical significance.

Insight into Local Customs and Folklore

To truly understand the essence of the Loire Valley, it is imperative to delve into its customs and folklore, as they provide a fascinating glimpse into the region's cultural heritage. The Loire Valley proudly showcases its traditions through a diverse array of events, allowing visitors to immerse themselves in the rich tapestry of local customs and practices.

One such event that offers a captivating insight into Loire Valley traditions is the Festival de la Saint-Martin in Tours. This annual celebration takes place during the harvest season, usually in November, and is dedicated to Saint Martin, the patron saint of winemakers. The festival brings together locals and visitors alike in a jubilant atmosphere of merriment. Colorful parades wind through the streets, accompanied by the vibrant sounds of traditional music. Witnessing the lively procession, adorned with costumes and floats, is a treat for the senses, as it highlights the deep-rooted connection between the people of the Loire Valley and their agricultural heritage.

Concerts featuring local musicians provide an opportunity to experience the enchanting melodies and rhythms that have been passed down through generations. The air is filled with the soul-stirring tunes of traditional instruments, bringing to life the spirit of the region. The Festival de la Saint-Martin is also renowned for its gastronomic delights, particularly the traditional Saint-Martin's goose feasts. This culinary tradition, rooted in history, showcases the region's culinary expertise and offers a chance to savor the rich flavors of Loire Valley cuisine.

Another festival that offers a unique window into Loire Valley customs is the Fête des Vendanges in Montlouis-sur-Loire. This lively event is dedicated to the grape harvest, a vital period in the region's winemaking calendar. During the festival, vineyards come alive with activity, and visitors have the opportunity to actively engage in winemaking traditions. Joining the grape stomping festivities allows participants to experience firsthand the age-old practice of crushing grapes with their feet, a symbolic and joyous act that symbolizes the beginning of the winemaking process.

As you explore the Fête des Vendanges, you'll gain a deeper understanding of the intricate craftsmanship and expertise involved in winemaking. Local vintners are often present, sharing their knowledge and passion for their craft. You'll learn about the different grape varieties, the art of vine cultivation, and the intricacies of the fermentation process.

Engaging in conversations with winemakers and tasting their creations offers a unique opportunity to appreciate the dedication and skill that go into producing the renowned wines of the Loire Valley.

Attending these festivals in the Loire Valley provides a multifaceted experience. It allows you to witness traditional dances, music, and storytelling that have been passed down through generations, providing a window into the cultural heritage of the region. By partaking in events like the Festival de la Saint-Martin and the Fête des Vendanges, you will forge a deeper connection with the Loire Valley and gain a profound appreciation for its customs, folklore, and the people who uphold these traditions with pride.

Participatory Experiences for Visitors

In the enchanting Loire Valley, the festivals and events go beyond mere spectatorship, offering visitors incredible opportunities to actively engage and immerse themselves in the local culture. These events provide a platform for hands-on experiences that showcase the region's traditional craftsmanship, interactive performances, and unique participatory activities that foster a deep connection with the local community.

One of the highlights of attending festivals in the Loire Valley is the chance to join workshops and demonstrations that highlight the region's rich artistic heritage. Discover the art of pottery making as skilled artisans guide you through the process of shaping clay into beautiful vessels. Learn the intricate techniques of weaving as you create your own masterpiece using traditional looms. Engage in the time-honored practice of bread baking, where you can knead dough, shape it into loaves, and witness the magic of transforming simple ingredients into delicious, freshly baked bread. These workshops not only allow you to learn new skills but also provide insights into the craftsmanship that has been cherished in the Loire Valley for centuries.

Immerse yourself further in the vibrant culture of the Loire Valley by taking part in interactive performances. Learn the steps of traditional dances, guided by local experts who share the rhythms and stories behind each movement. Pick up a musical instrument and join in a lively jam session, discovering the melodies and tunes that have echoed through the valleys for generations. For those with a love for history and adventure, try your hand at medieval archery, experiencing the thrill of mastering a skill practiced by knights of old. These interactive performances offer a window into the region's cultural traditions and allow you to embrace the rhythm and energy of the Loire Valley.

One of the standout events that epitomizes the participatory nature of the Loire Valley festivals is the Festivals of Loire in Orléans. This unique celebration provides a once-in-a-lifetime opportunity to navigate the majestic Loire River on a traditional boat. As you glide along the tranquil waters, surrounded by stunning landscapes, you'll witness the beauty of the region from a different perspective. Additionally, lively riverbank concerts fill the air with music, inviting you to dance, sing along, and join in the jubilant festivities. These immersive experiences allow you to forge connections with both the natural splendor of the Loire Valley and the local community, fostering a sense of belonging and creating memories that will endure.

In the Loire Valley, festivals and events are not just occasions to observe from the sidelines but invitations to actively participate and engage. Whether it's learning traditional crafts, joining in interactive performances, or embarking on unique adventures, these experiences offer a deeper understanding of the region's culture and heritage. By connecting with the local community, you become a part of the living tapestry that makes the Loire Valley so extraordinary, leaving you with indelible memories of a truly immersive and enriching journey.

Beyond the workshops, interactive performances, and unique activities, the participatory experiences at festivals and events in the Loire Valley offer even more opportunities for visitors to connect with the local community and create unforgettable memories.

As you engage in the various activities, you'll find yourself surrounded by friendly locals who are eager to share their stories, traditions, and knowledge. They warmly welcome you into their world, encouraging conversation and fostering cultural exchange. Whether it's a potter sharing the history and significance of their craft, a musician teaching you a traditional melody, or a festival-goer sharing their favorite local recipe, these interactions allow you to form genuine connections and gain deeper insights into the region's identity.

Participating in the Festivals of Loire in Orléans is a prime example of how these events facilitate community engagement. As you navigate the Loire River on a traditional boat, you'll encounter fellow travelers and locals alike, all united in their love for the region and its festivities. Conversations flow effortlessly, and you may find yourself swapping travel tips, exchanging cultural anecdotes, or simply reveling in the joyous atmosphere together. The shared experience of witnessing riverbank concerts creates a sense of camaraderie, as you cheer, dance, and sing alongside fellow revelers. These moments of connection transcend language barriers and cultural differences, reminding us of the universal language of celebration and shared joy.

Beyond the immediate enjoyment, participating in festivals and events also leaves a lasting impact. The skills you acquire during workshops become cherished mementos of your time in the Loire Valley, allowing you to carry a piece of its craftsmanship home with you. The dances you learn and the musical notes you play become cherished memories that you can revisit and share with others. The connections you forge with the local community become a bridge between cultures, inspiring a deeper appreciation for diversity and fostering a sense of global citizenship.

Moreover, these participatory experiences ignite a spark of curiosity and passion within you. They encourage you to explore further, to delve into the region's history, art, and culinary traditions. They motivate you to uncover hidden gems and off-the-beaten-path destinations, ensuring that your journey through the Loire Valley is not limited to the festival grounds alone.

In the Loire Valley, the festivals and events are gateways to a world of immersive experiences, cultural exchange, and lifelong connections. They go beyond mere entertainment, inviting you to actively engage, learn, and become part of the fabric of this captivating region. By embracing these participatory opportunities, you open yourself up to a profound and transformative travel experience that will stay with you long after you bid adieu to the Loire Valley.

By immersing yourself in the traditional festivals and events of the Loire Valley, you will gain a deeper appreciation for the region's cultural heritage. Whether you witness grand processions, learn about local customs and folklore, or actively participate in interactive experiences, these festivities will undoubtedly leave you with a profound understanding of the vibrant traditions that make the Loire Valley so captivating.

Chapter 3: Unforgettable Experiences

Exploring Natural Splendors

The Loire Valley is blessed with an abundance of natural beauty, and this chapter invites you to immerse yourself in the region's breathtaking landscapes and awe-inspiring natural splendors. From the tranquil Loire River to meticulously manicured gardens and opportunities for outdoor adventures, there's something for every nature enthusiast.

Loire River: The Lifeline of the Valley

Flowing gracefully through the heart of the Loire Valley, the Loire River is indeed the lifeline of the region, both historically and geographically. As you follow its meandering course, you'll be enchanted by the picturesque charm of the surrounding countryside. The river's banks are adorned with lush vineyards, where rows of grapevines stretch as far as the eye can see. The fertile soil and favorable climate have made the Loire Valley renowned for its exquisite wines, and the vineyards along the riverbanks are a testament to this proud tradition.

Along the Loire River, you'll also come across quaint villages and historic towns that seem to have been frozen in time. These idyllic settlements exude a peaceful ambiance, inviting you to explore their cobbled streets, half-timbered houses, and charming squares. Take a moment to immerse yourself in the local culture, perhaps by visiting a traditional market, savoring regional delicacies, or striking up conversations with friendly locals. The villages and towns along the Loire

River offer a glimpse into the region's rich history and provide a tranquil respite from the bustling modern world.

One of the best ways to experience the Loire River is by embarking on a leisurely boat cruise. Allow the gentle current to carry you along, as you soak in the stunning scenery that unfolds before your eyes. The riverbanks are adorned with an impressive array of architectural wonders, including magnificent châteaux that have withstood the test of time. These grand residences, each with its own unique story, showcase the opulence and elegance of bygone eras. From the iconic Château de Chambord with its Renaissance splendor to the graceful arches of Château de Chenonceau spanning the river itself, the Loire River offers a front-row seat to these captivating landmarks.

As you glide along the Loire River, you'll find yourself in an idyllic setting that inspires relaxation, contemplation, and appreciation of the surrounding beauty. The tranquil waters mirror the sky above, creating a sense of serenity that allows you to escape the worries of everyday life. Capture the mesmerizing landscapes with your camera, as the play of light and shadows accentuates the natural splendor. Whether you choose to bask in the sun's warm glow on the deck of a boat or find a peaceful spot along the riverbank, the Loire River offers a sanctuary for rejuvenation and a chance to reconnect with nature.

The Loire River truly embodies the essence of the Loire Valley, seamlessly blending natural beauty with cultural heritage. It is a symbol of the region's past, present, and future, and a source of inspiration for artists, writers, and travelers alike. As you explore its waters, you'll understand why the Loire River is often considered the lifeblood of the region, as it nourishes the land, shapes the landscape, and weaves together the many elements that make the Loire Valley a captivating destination.

The Loire River not only serves as a captivating backdrop for your journey through the Loire Valley but also provides an opportunity to engage with its rich ecosystem. The river is home to a diverse range of flora and fauna, and as you cruise along its gentle currents, you may spot graceful swans gliding on the water's surface or herons elegantly poised on the riverbanks. Keep an eye out for vibrant wildflowers that adorn the shores, adding bursts of color to the already scenic landscape.

For those seeking a deeper connection with the Loire River, various activities allow you to fully appreciate its significance. Consider joining a guided kayaking or canoeing expedition, allowing you to navigate the river at your own pace, immersing yourself in its tranquility. Paddling along the Loire River offers a unique perspective, allowing you to explore hidden coves, discover secluded islands, and observe the river's flora and fauna up close.

Fishing enthusiasts will find ample opportunities to cast their lines into the Loire River's waters. Known for its diverse fish population, the river is a haven for anglers seeking a peaceful day by the water. Whether you prefer fly fishing or traditional rod and reel, the Loire River presents a chance to reel in species such as pike, perch, carp, and trout, providing a memorable angling experience amid the natural beauty of the region.

Beyond the river itself, the Loire Valley boasts an array of natural reserves, islands, and wetlands that are worth exploring. Nature enthusiasts can venture into these protected areas, such as the National Nature Reserve of Saint-Mesmin or the Brenne Regional Nature Park, to witness a myriad of bird species, lush vegetation, and untouched habitats. These reserves offer opportunities for birdwatching, nature walks, and guided tours, allowing you to deepen your understanding of the Loire Valley's ecological importance.

Whether you choose to observe the Loire River from the comfort of a boat, paddle its waters in a kayak, or explore the surrounding natural reserves, the river's presence will undoubtedly enhance your experience of the Loire Valley. It serves as a constant reminder of the region's interconnectedness with nature and its ability to provide both solace and inspiration. So, let the Loire River be your guide as you traverse the stunning landscapes of the Loire Valley, leaving you with lasting memories of a journey shaped by the beauty and vitality of this lifeline of the region.

Gardens and Parks: Serenity Amidst Beauty

The Loire Valley's gardens and parks are a testament to the region's dedication to preserving its natural heritage and creating captivating spaces for visitors to enjoy. As you step into these enchanting landscapes, you'll find yourself immersed in a world of beauty and tranquility.

One of the most renowned gardens in the Loire Valley is Villandry, known for its impeccable design and breathtaking beauty. As you wander through Villandry's gardens, you'll encounter meticulously shaped hedges, perfectly manicured lawns, and vibrant flower beds. What sets Villandry apart are its famous geometric patterns, created with various colored flowers, forming intricate designs that are truly a sight to behold. The garden's pièce de résistance is its impressive vegetable garden, where a stunning array of vegetables and herbs are cultivated in harmonious rows. This unique blend of aesthetics and functionality makes Villandry a must-visit for horticulture enthusiasts and those seeking inspiration.

Another gem among the Loire Valley's gardens is the Château de Chaumont. Here, nature and contemporary art come together in perfect harmony. As you explore the Château de Chaumont's grounds, you'll encounter thought-provoking art installations nestled amidst the serene surroundings. The juxtaposition of sculptures, installations, and landscaping elements creates a captivating experience, where art and nature intertwine. With its rich history and innovative approach to blending art and natural beauty, Château de Chaumont's gardens offer a unique and inspiring journey for visitors.

For a more serene and panoramic experience, the Jardins de Château d'Amboise provides a peaceful oasis with breathtaking views of the Loire Valley. Nestled near the Château d'Amboise, these gardens offer a place of respite and contemplation. Take a leisurely stroll through the garden's paths, lined with vibrant flower beds, fragrant shrubs, and ancient trees. As you wander, you'll be rewarded with sweeping vistas of the valley below, showcasing the Loire River meandering through the picturesque landscape. Whether you choose to find a quiet bench to reflect upon the beauty around you or simply take in the panoramic views, Jardins de Château d'Amboise invites you to embrace a sense of peace and serenity.

In addition to Villandry, Château de Chaumont, and Jardins de Château d'Amboise, the Loire Valley boasts a multitude of other remarkable gardens and parks, each with its own unique charm and character.

The Château de Chenonceau is home to exquisite gardens that perfectly complement the elegance of the château itself.

Stroll through the Renaissance Garden, where flower beds bloom with vibrant colors and fragrant blooms. As you wander further, you'll encounter the serene Water Garden, adorned with graceful arches and tranquil reflecting pools. The combination of meticulously manicured landscapes and the château's reflection in the water creates an ethereal and romantic atmosphere, making it a favorite among visitors.

For a taste of Japanese-inspired tranquility, make your way to the Domaine Régional de Chaumont-sur-Loire. Here, you'll find the Garden of Metamorphoses, a serene space that blends Japanese garden design principles with local flora. Meandering paths, stone lanterns, and serene ponds filled with koi fish create a peaceful ambiance, inviting visitors to slow down and appreciate the beauty of nature. The garden's sense of harmony and balance offers a peaceful respite amidst the Loire Valley's cultural richness.

If you're seeking a unique and immersive experience, the International Garden Festival at the Domaine de Chaumont-sur-Loire is a must-visit. Each year, landscape architects and designers from around the world create captivating and thought-provoking garden installations, showcasing innovative ideas and pushing the boundaries of traditional garden design. From avant-garde concepts to sustainable practices, the festival invites visitors to explore the cutting-edge of garden artistry and find inspiration in the fusion of nature and creativity.

Beyond these notable gardens, the Loire Valley is also home to numerous public parks and green spaces that offer opportunities for relaxation and leisure. Parc de la Perraudière in Tours, for example, provides a peaceful escape from the city's bustle, featuring beautiful flower beds, walking paths, and recreational facilities. Parc Balzac in

Angers offers a serene environment with shaded areas, picturesque ponds, and even a charming little island. These parks are ideal for picnics, leisurely walks, or simply finding a quiet spot to soak up the beauty of nature.

Whether you're a dedicated garden enthusiast, an art lover, or someone who appreciates the serenity of nature, the Loire Valley's gardens and parks offer a captivating journey through carefully crafted landscapes and a deep connection with the region's natural heritage. From the symmetrical beauty of Villandry to the harmonious blend of contemporary art and nature at Château de Chaumont, each garden and park invites you to slow down, indulge your senses, and create lasting memories amidst the beauty of the Loire Valley.

Outdoor Activities: Cycling, Hiking, and More

For those seeking a more active experience, the Loire Valley offers a plethora of outdoor activities that cater to a variety of interests and fitness levels. The region's scenic landscapes provide the perfect backdrop for engaging in thrilling adventures and immersing oneself in the natural wonders of the area.

Cycling enthusiasts will find themselves in paradise as they pedal along well-marked routes that meander through the Loire Valley's picturesque countryside. These cycling paths lead you through vineyards, where you can catch glimpses of grapevines stretching as far as the eye can see, producing the renowned wines that the region is famous for. As you pedal past sunflower fields, you'll be captivated by the vibrant golden hues that blanket the landscape. The routes also take you through charming villages, allowing you to discover hidden gems and interact with the friendly locals. Whether you're an avid cyclist or a leisurely rider, the cycling trails in the Loire Valley offer a delightful way to explore the region at your own pace.

If you prefer to explore on foot, the Loire Valley presents an extensive network of hiking trails that crisscross the valley. Lace up your hiking boots and embark on an adventure that unveils breathtaking vistas and encounters with nature. Whether you opt for a gentle stroll along the riverbanks or a more challenging hike up the rolling hills, there are trails suited to all levels of fitness and expertise. As you ascend to higher vantage points, you'll be rewarded with panoramic views of the undulating landscapes, the Loire River winding through the valley, and the impressive châteaux that dot the horizon. Along the way, keep an eye out for native flora and fauna, adding an element of wildlife appreciation to your hike. The trails in the Loire Valley offer a chance to disconnect from the hustle and bustle of everyday life and reconnect with the tranquility of nature.

For water enthusiasts, the Loire River presents a playground for aquatic adventures. Kayaking and canoeing are popular activities that allow you to explore the waterways that define the region. Glide along the gentle currents of the Loire River, taking in the serene surroundings as you navigate through the heart of the valley. Paddle past lush greenery, ancient bridges, and riverside hamlets, immersing yourself in the beauty of the natural environment. Fishing enthusiasts will also find solace in the Loire River, casting their lines and patiently waiting for the catch of the day. Whether you choose to paddle, fish, or simply bask in the tranquility of the river, the Loire's water-based activities provide a unique perspective and an opportunity to forge a deeper connection with the region's aquatic ecosystems.

Engaging in these outdoor adventures not only offers physical benefits but also allows you to develop a profound appreciation for the natural wonders that make the Loire Valley so remarkable. As you cycle through vineyards, hike along scenic trails, or explore the waterways, you'll witness firsthand the harmonious coexistence of the region's cultural heritage and its pristine landscapes. The interplay between the châteaux, vineyards, and natural beauty creates an enchanting tapestry that is unique to the Loire Valley. Embrace the active side of your journey, and let the outdoor experiences in the Loire Valley leave an indelible mark on your travel memories.

Immersing yourself in the outdoor activities of the Loire Valley goes beyond the physical aspects. It offers a chance to connect with the rich history and cultural traditions that have shaped the region for centuries. As you cycle through the vineyards, you'll gain insight into the winemaking heritage that has made the Loire Valley renowned for its exquisite wines. You may even have the opportunity to stop at local wineries, where passionate vintners will eagerly share their knowledge and offer tastings of their finest vintages.

While hiking along the trails, you'll not only be treated to breathtaking views but also have the chance to stumble upon hidden treasures tucked away in the valley. Serendipitous encounters with historic ruins, ancient chapels, and charming cottages add a sense of discovery and intrigue to your outdoor excursions. These chance encounters provide glimpses into the region's past and the lives of those who have called the Loire Valley home.

Moreover, the outdoor activities in the Loire Valley foster a deep appreciation for the region's commitment to environmental preservation. As you cycle, hike, or paddle, you'll witness the conservation efforts undertaken to protect the natural habitats and promote sustainable practices. From eco-friendly cycling paths to the preservation of biodiversity in the river ecosystem, the Loire Valley sets an example of responsible tourism and the harmonious coexistence of humans and nature.

Engaging in outdoor adventures also allows for meaningful connections with fellow travelers and locals alike. Along the cycling routes or hiking trails, you may encounter like-minded explorers who share your love for nature and adventure. Friendly exchanges, shared tips, and stories of memorable experiences create a sense of camaraderie and a chance to forge new friendships. Meanwhile, encounters with the locals provide opportunities to learn about their way of life, traditions, and the deep-rooted connection they have with the land.

By indulging in the outdoor activities offered by the Loire Valley, you'll find yourself fully immersed in the region's beauty, history, and culture. From the vibrant vineyards to the tranquil river, every moment spent exploring the natural splendors becomes an unforgettable experience that deepens your understanding of this captivating destination. So, lace up your shoes, hop on a bicycle, or pick up a paddle – embark on an adventure that will leave you with cherished memories and a profound appreciation for the remarkable wonders of the Loire Valley.

The Loire Valley is not just about magnificent châteaux and cultural heritage but also about connecting with nature. Whether you choose to meander along the Loire River, find tranquility in the enchanting gardens and parks, or embark on outdoor activities like cycling and hiking, the natural splendors of the Loire Valley will leave an indelible mark on your travel memories.

Off the Beaten Path: Hidden Gems and Rural Charms

The Loire Valley is not only famous for its grand châteaux and stunning landscapes but also for its hidden gems and rural charms. In this chapter, we will take you on a journey to discover the lesser-known attractions and experiences that showcase the authentic essence of the region.

Quaint Villages and Historic Towns

Venture away from the well-trodden tourist paths and explore the picturesque villages and historic towns scattered throughout the Loire Valley. These hidden gems offer a glimpse into the region's rich history and local traditions. Visit:

Montrésor:

Montrésor, located in the Indre department of the Loire Valley, is a hidden gem that has earned its reputation as one of the "Most Beautiful Villages of France." This picturesque village offers a delightful escape into a world of timeless beauty and enchanting medieval architecture.

As you wander through Montrésor's cobblestone streets, you'll be transported back in time. The village's well-preserved medieval architecture is truly a sight to behold. Immerse yourself in the ambiance as you admire the charming half-timbered houses adorned with colorful flowers, intricate carvings, and wooden shutters.

A highlight of any visit to Montrésor is a visit to the Château de Montrésor. This stunning castle, perched on a rocky hill overlooking the village, dates back to the 11th century. Step inside and explore its rich history and architectural splendor. Marvel at the imposing towers, graceful turrets, and the intricate details that tell the stories of bygone eras.

As you explore the château, you'll have the opportunity to discover its various rooms, including the grand salon, chapel, and the medieval kitchen. Admire the beautiful tapestries, antique furniture, and period artwork that adorn the interiors. From the castle's ramparts, take in panoramic views of the village, the surrounding countryside, and the Indrois River, which gracefully winds its way through the landscape.

Beyond the château, Montrésor offers a serene and peaceful atmosphere. Take a leisurely stroll along the riverbanks or through the village's charming gardens. Enjoy the tranquility of the Place des Douves, a square surrounded by ancient stone walls, or visit the Church of Saint-Jean-Baptiste, an architectural gem dating back to the 12th century.

For those interested in the arts, Montrésor is also home to a vibrant artistic community. Explore local art galleries and studios, where you can discover the works of talented painters, sculptors, and artisans who find inspiration in the village's beauty.

To fully immerse yourself in Montrésor's charm, consider indulging in the local gastronomy. Visit the village's quaint cafes and restaurants, where you can savor regional specialties and traditional French cuisine. Pair your meal with a glass of local wine, and let the flavors of the Loire Valley tantalize your taste buds.

A visit to Montrésor is a journey into the past, an opportunity to experience the beauty and tranquility of a quintessential French village. Whether you're captivated by its medieval architecture, enchanted by its natural surroundings, or simply seeking a peaceful retreat, Montrésor promises an unforgettable experience in the heart of the Loire Valley.

Lavardin:

Lavardin, a small village perched on a hilltop overlooking the meandering Loir River, is a true gem in the Loire Valley. As you approach Lavardin, you'll be captivated by the sight of its ancient stone houses and the impressive ruins of its 12th-century castle.

Stepping into Lavardin feels like stepping back in time. The village exudes an old-world charm with its narrow lanes, cobblestone streets, and well-preserved medieval architecture. As you take a leisurely walk through the village, you'll be enchanted by the peaceful atmosphere that surrounds you.

One of the highlights of Lavardin is undoubtedly its castle ruin. The imposing remains of the 12th-century fortress stand as a testament to the village's rich history. As you explore the castle grounds, you can envision the grandeur and power it once held. Climb to the highest point of the ruins and be rewarded with breathtaking panoramic views of the surrounding countryside. The sweeping vistas of lush green fields, rolling hills, and the meandering Loir River below create a picturesque scene that is sure to leave you in awe.

Beyond the castle, Lavardin offers more hidden treasures to discover. Explore the charming streets lined with beautifully restored stone houses, many of which have stood for centuries. Admire the intricate details of the architecture, from the ornate doorways to the decorative window shutters. Lavardin's residents take great pride in maintaining the authenticity of their village, and their efforts shine through in every corner.

During your stroll, you'll encounter small artisan shops and galleries, offering a glimpse into the local creativity and craftsmanship. Take the opportunity to browse unique handmade crafts, artwork, and locally produced goods, making for perfect souvenirs to remember your time in Lavardin.

If you're seeking a moment of tranquility, find a cozy café or a bench along the riverbank, and simply soak in the peaceful ambiance. The gentle sounds of the Loir River flowing by and the distant chirping of birds create a serene backdrop that invites you to relax and embrace the beauty of the surroundings.

Lavardin's charm lies not only in its physical beauty but also in its sense of timelessness. It is a place where history comes alive, and the slower pace of life allows you to appreciate the simple pleasures. Whether you choose to wander aimlessly through its narrow lanes, explore the castle ruins, or simply take in the panoramic views, Lavardin is a captivating village that will leave an indelible mark on your heart and soul.

Beaugency:

Beaugency is a captivating historic town nestled on the banks of the picturesque Loire River. Stepping into Beaugency is like taking a leap back in time, as its well-preserved medieval center exudes an enchanting atmosphere that will transport you to a bygone era.

The heart of Beaugency is its charming medieval center, where winding cobblestone streets and half-timbered houses evoke a sense of medieval splendor. As you explore the narrow lanes, you'll encounter architectural marvels that showcase the town's rich heritage. The highlight of Beaugency's historic center is the magnificent Saint-Étienne Church, an impressive Gothic structure that stands as a testament to the town's spiritual and architectural significance. Step inside to admire its intricate stained glass windows, soaring vaulted ceilings, and ornate stone carvings.

One of the most iconic landmarks in Beaugency is its stone bridge, known as the "Pont de Beaugency." This bridge spans across the Loire River, offering breathtaking panoramic views of the town and the tranquil waters below. Take a leisurely stroll across the bridge and pause to soak in the beauty of the surrounding landscape. The bridge itself is a remarkable architectural feat, with its arches reflecting in the gentle ripples of the river.

In addition to its architectural treasures, Beaugency also boasts a rich history that can be discovered through its museums and heritage sites. Visit the Maison de Beauce, a museum dedicated to the region's agricultural heritage, to learn about the traditional farming practices that have shaped the landscape. The Musée d'Histoire et d'Archéologie de Beaugency provides insights into the town's past through its collection of archaeological artifacts and historical exhibits.

As you explore Beaugency, you'll find a delightful array of cafes, restaurants, and shops that invite you to indulge in local cuisine and browse for unique souvenirs. Sample traditional delicacies such as the famous rillettes or enjoy a leisurely meal while savoring the charming ambiance of the town.

Beaugency is also an ideal base for further exploration of the Loire Valley. From here, you can embark on scenic walks or bike rides along the river, discovering hidden trails and beautiful landscapes. Additionally, the town hosts various events and festivals throughout the year, providing an opportunity to immerse yourself in the local culture and traditions.

Whether you are drawn to its medieval allure, panoramic vistas, or cultural heritage, Beaugency offers a truly captivating experience. It is a place where history comes alive, inviting you to wander its streets, soak up its ambiance, and create unforgettable memories of your journey through the enchanting Loire Valley.

Rural Life and Authentic Encounters

To truly immerse yourself in the Loire Valley's charm, venture into the rural areas and experience authentic encounters with the locals. Engage in activities that offer a glimpse into traditional life and showcase the region's agricultural heritage. Here are some suggestions:

Farm Visits:

Immerse yourself in the agricultural heritage of the Loire Valley by spending a day at a working farm. These visits provide a unique opportunity to learn about the sustainable agricultural practices that sustain the region's renowned produce. Depending on the season and the farm you visit, you can participate in a range of hands-on activities.

If you visit a dairy farm, you can try your hand at cheese-making, guided by experienced artisans who will teach you the art of transforming milk into delicious cheeses. You'll gain insights into the traditional methods used and learn about the different types of cheese produced in the region. From goat cheese to renowned varieties like Sainte-Maure-de-Touraine or Crottin de Chavignol, you'll have the chance to savor the flavors and understand the craftsmanship behind each creation.

During the grape harvest season, you can join in the exhilarating process of wine production. Engage in picking grapes, experience the vineyards' vibrant atmosphere, and witness the initial stages of winemaking. Knowledgeable vintners will guide you through the process, sharing their expertise on grape varieties, vineyard management, and the art of winemaking. Of course, no farm visit would be complete without a wine tasting session, where you can savor the distinct flavors of the Loire Valley's renowned wines, including crisp Sauvignon Blancs, elegant Chenin Blancs, and delicious reds like Cabernet Franc.

If you visit during the harvest season for fruits such as apples, pears, or cherries, you can engage in fruit picking, experiencing the joy of plucking ripe and succulent produce directly from the orchards. This hands-on experience allows you to connect with nature and appreciate the freshness and flavor of locally grown fruits.

Throughout these farm visits, you'll have the opportunity to interact with farmers who are deeply connected to the land. They will share their knowledge, stories, and passion for their craft, offering a genuine insight into their way of life and the challenges and joys of working in agriculture. By the end of your farm visit, you'll not only have a greater appreciation for the region's agricultural practices but also for the hard work and dedication of the farmers who sustain the Loire Valley's bounty.

Local Markets:

One of the best ways to immerse yourself in the local culture and flavors of the Loire Valley is by exploring the vibrant markets that dot various towns and villages throughout the week. These markets provide a lively atmosphere, bustling with locals and visitors alike, all seeking to indulge in the region's gastronomic delights and discover unique artisanal crafts.

As you stroll through the market stalls, your senses will be invigorated by the colorful array of fresh produce. From plump tomatoes and fragrant herbs to juicy berries and the famous Loire Valley asparagus, the variety of seasonal fruits and vegetables is a testament to the region's fertile soils. Take the opportunity to sample some of these delights, savoring their flavors and experiencing the true essence of local produce.

Beyond the fresh produce, you'll find a treasure trove of regional specialties. Indulge in artisanal cheeses, handmade chocolates, and cured meats crafted by skilled artisans. Discover jars of homemade jams, jellies, and honey, each one representing the distinct flavors of the Loire Valley's flora. Don't forget to explore the array of local wines and spirits, allowing your taste buds to savor the region's vinicultural heritage.

Apart from the culinary offerings, local markets are also a hub for artisanal crafts and unique souvenirs. You'll find talented artisans showcasing their skills through pottery, glassware, jewelry, textiles, and more. These handicrafts often reflect the region's rich history and artistic traditions, making them perfect mementos of your journey through the Loire Valley.

Mingling with the locals at the market offers a chance to engage in conversations and forge connections with the people who call the region home. You can strike up conversations with the vendors, who are passionate about their products and eager to share their knowledge and recommendations. They can provide insights into the cultural significance of certain dishes, suggest the best ways to enjoy local specialties, and even share recipes passed down through generations.

The market atmosphere itself is a vibrant and bustling experience. As you navigate the lively crowds, you'll witness the energy and liveliness that these gatherings bring to the towns and villages. Street musicians may serenade the visitors, adding a melodic backdrop to your exploration. Children might be entertained by puppet shows or face painting, adding an extra layer of joy to the ambiance.

Attending a local market in the Loire Valley is not just about shopping and sampling, but also about embracing the sense of community that thrives within these gatherings. You'll see friends catching up over a cup of coffee, neighbors exchanging news and stories, and generations coming together to celebrate their shared heritage.

Festivals and Rural Celebrations:

The Loire Valley is deeply rooted in its traditions and rural customs, which are celebrated throughout the year in various festivals and rural celebrations. Keeping an eye out for these events will allow you to witness age-old traditions and immerse yourself in the vibrant cultural tapestry of the region.

Traditional festivals often showcase a combination of music, dance, gastronomy, and cultural exhibitions. Whether it's a village fête, a harvest festival, or a celebration of a local saint, these events bring the community together in a spirited atmosphere.

Gastronomy takes center stage during these celebrations, as local delicacies are prepared and enjoyed. You can savor the unique flavors of the Loire Valley's culinary heritage, including regional specialties such as rillettes (pork pâté), fouées (small baked bread pockets), and tarte Tatin (caramelized apple tart). It's an opportunity to indulge in the tastes and aromas that define the local cuisine.

Music and dance performances play a significant role in rural celebrations. Folklore groups may showcase traditional dances and costumes, while local musicians serenade the crowd with lively tunes. These performances provide a glimpse into the cultural heritage and artistic expressions that have shaped the identity of the Loire Valley.

Attending these festivals and rural celebrations allows you to join in the festivities alongside the locals, forging connections and creating shared memories. It's a chance to witness the rich tapestry of customs and traditions that make the Loire Valley a captivating destination.

By engaging in farm visits, exploring local markets, and joining festivals and rural celebrations, you'll deepen your connection to the authentic essence of the Loire Valley. These experiences provide a window into the region's agricultural heritage, culinary delights, and vibrant cultural traditions, ensuring that your journey through the Loire Valley is filled with unforgettable moments and a true sense of immersion.

Lesser-Known Attractions and Excursions

Beyond the famous châteaux, the Loire Valley is dotted with hidden attractions and off-the-beaten-path excursions that promise unique experiences. Consider adding these lesser-known gems to your itinerary:

Caves of Rochemenier:

Deep beneath the surface of the town of Louresse-Rochemenier lies an extraordinary attraction known as the Caves of Rochemenier. This unique site allows visitors to step back in time and discover an underground village that was once inhabited by local peasants. As you venture into the labyrinthine network of troglodyte dwellings, you'll be transported to a bygone era and gain fascinating insights into the lives of those who once called these caves home.

Exploring the Caves of Rochemenier is like entering a hidden world. The cool, dimly lit chambers reveal the rustic simplicity of the past, with rooms carved out of the soft limestone walls. Wander through the interconnected spaces, each one telling a story of its own. Observe the modest living quarters, the stone-carved fireplaces, and the crude but functional furniture that provided comfort to the villagers.

The caves offer more than just a glimpse into the living conditions of the past. Informative exhibits and displays provide a deeper understanding of the history and culture of the local community. Learn about the challenges and ingenuity of the inhabitants as they adapted to the unique environment of the underground village.

Puy du Fou:

While Puy du Fou is located outside the Loire Valley, it is undoubtedly a destination well worth the visit for history enthusiasts and families alike. This exceptional historical theme park takes visitors on a captivating journey through time, bringing key moments in history to life through immersive shows and experiences.

Step into the ancient Roman Empire and witness the thrilling spectacle of gladiators in combat. Marvel at the breathtaking feats of knights in full armor during the medieval period. Immerse yourself in the pageantry and drama of reenactments that depict pivotal events, from Viking invasions to the French Revolution. The attention to detail, elaborate sets, and talented performers create an atmosphere that is both educational and awe-inspiring.

Puy du Fou goes beyond mere entertainment; it aims to provide a comprehensive experience that educates and engages visitors of all ages. The park's dedication to historical accuracy is evident in every aspect, from the meticulously crafted costumes to the meticulously recreated historical settings. Interactive workshops and exhibits allow guests to delve deeper into specific time periods and crafts, providing a hands-on learning experience.

Mushroom Caves of Saumur:

Delve into the fascinating underground world of mushroom cultivation in the town of Saumur, where the Mushroom Caves offer a unique and educational experience. These underground caves, carved out of the tuffeau stone that characterizes the region, provide the ideal environment for cultivating mushrooms.

Embark on a guided tour through the labyrinthine passages of the Mushroom Caves and learn about the intricacies of mushroom cultivation. Expert guides will explain the various stages of cultivation, from the preparation of the growing beds to the harvesting process. Gain insight into the techniques used to cultivate different varieties of mushrooms and discover the importance of temperature, humidity, and air circulation in creating the optimal conditions for growth.

As you explore the Mushroom Caves, you'll encounter vast chambers filled with rows upon rows of mushroom beds. Marvel at the sight of the mushrooms in various stages of development, from tiny pinheads to fully grown specimens. The earthy aroma and the gentle sound of dripping water create a serene atmosphere as you immerse yourself in this hidden underground world.

After the tour, indulge your taste buds with the flavors of the mushrooms by sampling some delicious mushroom-based dishes. Local chefs often incorporate fresh mushrooms from the caves into their culinary creations, offering a unique and gastronomic experience that celebrates the region's rich agricultural heritage.

The Mushroom Caves of Saumur provide a fascinating blend of natural beauty, agricultural ingenuity, and culinary delight, making it a must-visit destination for those seeking a truly unique experience in the Loire Valley.

By exploring these hidden gems and embracing the rural charms of the Loire Valley, you will gain a deeper appreciation for the region's diverse offerings and create lasting memories of your journey.

Chapter 4: Practicalities and Resources

Planning Your Trip to the Loire Valley

When it comes to planning your trip to the Loire Valley, there are a few key considerations that can enhance your experience and make your visit more enjoyable. In this chapter, we will explore the best time to visit, the recommended duration of stay, transportation options, and various accommodation choices.

Best Time to Visit and Duration of Stay

The Loire Valley, with its diverse landscapes and rich cultural heritage, is a destination that can be enjoyed year-round. Each season in the Loire Valley has its own unique charm, offering visitors different experiences and attractions.

The spring and summer months, from April to September, are the most popular time to visit the Loire Valley. During this period, the weather is typically mild and pleasant, making it ideal for outdoor activities and exploring the region's enchanting châteaux and gardens. The landscapes come alive with vibrant colors as flowers bloom, creating a picturesque backdrop for your adventures. However, it's important to note that this is also the peak tourist season, so expect larger crowds at popular attractions. It is advisable to book accommodations and tickets in advance to secure your preferred choices.

If you prefer a quieter experience and don't mind cooler temperatures, the shoulder seasons of spring (April to June) and autumn (September to October) can be excellent alternatives. During these months, the weather is still pleasant, and you'll have the opportunity to witness the beauty of blooming flowers in spring or the stunning autumn foliage in fall. Additionally, the number of tourists tends to be lower compared to the peak season, allowing for a more relaxed and intimate experience. You can explore the châteaux and landscapes at a leisurely pace, appreciating the tranquility and serenity of the region.

The duration of your stay in the Loire Valley depends on your interests and the number of attractions you wish to explore. While it's possible to visit the major châteaux and experience the cultural and natural highlights in a shorter timeframe, a minimum of three to four days is recommended to fully immerse yourself in the essence of the region. This timeframe allows you to visit the iconic châteaux, wander through charming villages, indulge in local cuisine, and experience the natural beauty of the Loire River. However, if you have more time available, extending your stay to a week or more will enable you to delve deeper into the area. You can discover lesser-known sites, explore off-the-beaten-path destinations, engage in outdoor activities such as cycling along the Loire River, and truly absorb the local ambiance.

Ultimately, whether you choose to visit during the popular spring and summer months or opt for a quieter experience in the shoulder seasons, and regardless of the duration of your stay, the Loire Valley promises a captivating journey filled with history, natural splendor, and cultural delights.

Transportation and Getting Around

The Loire Valley is conveniently located in central France and offers several transportation options for travelers.

By Air:

The nearest international airports to the Loire Valley are Paris Charles de Gaulle Airport and Paris Orly Airport, both of which are well-connected to major cities worldwide. Upon arrival at either of these airports, travelers have the option to continue their journey to the Loire Valley by taking a domestic flight to Tours Val de Loire Airport, which serves as the primary gateway to the region.

Tours Val de Loire Airport is located approximately 6 kilometers (3.7 miles) north-northeast of the city of Tours, making it easily accessible for travelers heading to the Loire Valley. Several airlines operate domestic flights to Tours Val de Loire Airport from Paris, providing convenient connections for international travelers.

From Paris Charles de Gaulle Airport or Paris Orly Airport, there are regular domestic flights to Tours Val de Loire Airport throughout the day, with a flight duration of approximately one hour. It is advisable to check the flight schedules and book your tickets in advance to secure the best fares and ensure availability, especially during peak travel seasons.

Upon arrival at Tours Val de Loire Airport, various transportation options are available to reach your desired destination within the Loire Valley. The airport provides car rental services, allowing travelers to easily rent a vehicle and embark on a self-guided exploration of the region. Additionally, taxis and airport shuttles are readily available to transport visitors to their accommodations or preferred destinations.

For those who prefer not to rent a car, public transportation options are also accessible from Tours Val de Loire Airport. Bus services connect the airport to the city of Tours and surrounding towns, providing convenient access to popular attractions and transportation hubs. The buses are well-coordinated with the flight arrivals and departures, ensuring a seamless transfer for travelers.

Tours Val de Loire Airport offers modern facilities and amenities, including car parking, passenger services, and dining options, making it a convenient and comfortable starting point for your Loire Valley adventure. Whether you choose to fly directly to Tours Val de Loire Airport or include it as a stopover on your journey, this airport serves as an efficient gateway to the rich cultural heritage, breathtaking landscapes, and architectural wonders of the Loire Valley.

By Train:

Trains are an excellent way to reach the Loire Valley from Paris or other major cities in France. The French rail system, known as the SNCF, provides efficient and comfortable train services that connect various towns in the Loire Valley with Paris and other major cities.

The TGV (Train à Grande Vitesse), France's high-speed train network, offers quick and convenient connections to the Loire Valley. Departing from Paris, the TGV provides fast and direct routes to several key towns in the region, including Tours, Angers, and Orléans.

Tours: As one of the main gateways to the Loire Valley, Tours is a vibrant city that serves as an excellent starting point for exploring the region. Known for its rich history, charming streets, and proximity to numerous châteaux, Tours offers a great introduction to the Loire Valley experience. The TGV trains from Paris Montparnasse station to Tours provide a swift and comfortable journey, taking approximately 1 to 1.5 hours, depending on the train and route. The frequency of trains is quite high, with multiple departures throughout the day, allowing for flexibility in planning your travel. Upon arrival in Tours, you'll find a well-connected local transportation network, including buses and trams, making it easy to navigate the city and reach nearby attractions.

Angers: Situated in the western part of the Loire Valley, Angers is a captivating city known for its impressive medieval castle, the Château d'Angers, and its charming old town. The TGV trains from Paris Montparnasse station to Angers offer convenient connections to this cultural hub. The travel time from Paris to Angers typically ranges from 1.5 to 2 hours, depending on the train and route. Similar to Tours, there are several departures daily, providing flexibility for travelers. Once in Angers, you can explore the picturesque streets, visit the famous castle and tapestry, and indulge in the local gastronomy, which includes renowned wines and delicious regional specialties.

Orléans: Situated on the eastern edge of the Loire Valley, Orléans is a city with a rich history and a blend of traditional and modern elements. Known for its association with Joan of Arc, Orléans offers a fascinating mix of architectural wonders and cultural heritage. The TGV trains from Paris Austerlitz station to Orléans make the journey quick and convenient, with a travel time of approximately 1 hour. The frequency of trains is good, allowing for convenient travel options throughout the day. Upon arrival in Orléans, you can explore the charming old town, stroll along the banks of the Loire River, and visit notable sites such as the Cathédrale Sainte-Croix and the Maison de Jeanne d'Arc.

The TGV trains provide a comfortable and smooth journey, with onboard amenities such as spacious seating, power outlets, and sometimes Wi-Fi connectivity. It's advisable to book your train tickets in advance, especially during peak travel seasons, to secure the best fares and ensure availability.

Once you arrive at your destination in the Loire Valley, local transportation options, such as buses and taxis, are available to take you to your desired location, whether it's your hotel, a château, or a specific attraction. Many towns in the region have well-connected local train stations, making it easy to explore the surrounding areas without a car.

Traveling by train not only offers convenience and efficiency but also allows you to enjoy the scenic beauty of the French countryside as you journey through the Loire Valley. It's a stress-free and environmentally-friendly way to reach this captivating region and start your exploration of its magnificent châteaux, picturesque landscapes, and rich cultural heritage.

By Car:

Renting a car gives you the flexibility to explore the Loire Valley at your own pace and is a popular choice among visitors. The region is well-served by a network of highways, making it convenient to travel between different towns and châteaux.

Major car rental companies can be found at the airports and train stations in the Loire Valley, offering a wide range of vehicle options to suit your needs. It is advisable to book your car rental in advance, especially during the peak tourist season, to ensure availability and secure the best rates.

Having a car allows you to create your own itinerary and explore the Loire Valley's attractions at your leisure. You can easily reach the famous châteaux that are scattered throughout the region, such as Château de Chambord, Château de Chenonceau, and Château de Blois. The highways provide efficient connections between these landmarks, enabling you to plan your visits according to your interests and preferences.

In addition to the châteaux, the Loire Valley is renowned for its picturesque countryside, charming villages, and vineyards. Renting a car allows you to venture off the beaten path and discover hidden gems that may not be easily accessible by public transportation. You can take scenic drives along the Loire River, explore quaint villages like Amboise or Saumur, and visit local wineries to sample the region's famous wines.

While driving in the Loire Valley, it is important to familiarize yourself with the local traffic rules and regulations. Speed limits are strictly enforced, and it's essential to always have your driver's license, rental documentation, and insurance information on hand. It is also recommended to have a GPS or a reliable navigation app to assist you in finding your way around.

Parking is generally available in most towns and cities in the Loire Valley. Many of the châteaux have designated parking areas for visitors. However, during peak tourist periods, these parking lots can become crowded, so it's advisable to arrive early to secure a spot.

It's worth noting that while renting a car offers convenience and flexibility, it may not be the most suitable option for everyone. If you prefer not to drive or are looking for a more sustainable mode of transportation, the Loire Valley also offers alternatives such as public buses and trains. These options can be particularly useful if you plan to focus on specific areas or if you prefer to avoid the responsibility of navigating and parking a vehicle.

Ultimately, whether you choose to rent a car or opt for other modes of transportation, the Loire Valley's well-connected highways and transportation infrastructure ensure that you can easily explore the region's diverse attractions, immerse yourself in its rich cultural heritage, and create lasting memories of your visit.

Public Transportation:

Within the Loire Valley, you'll find a reliable and convenient public transportation network that can help you navigate the region with ease. The two primary modes of public transportation in the Loire Valley are buses and local trains, each serving different purposes and catering to different travel needs.

Buses: Buses are an excellent and cost-effective way to reach smaller towns and villages within the Loire Valley. They provide essential connections between various destinations, including those that may not be easily accessible by train. Bus services are well-organized and operated by reliable companies, offering regular schedules and comfortable rides.

When using buses, it's important to familiarize yourself with the bus routes and timetables in advance. Local tourist offices or transportation centers can provide you with maps, schedules, and information on fares. Keep in mind that bus services may be less frequent during weekends and holidays, so plan your trips accordingly.

Buses are particularly convenient for visiting off-the-beaten-path attractions, rural areas, and picturesque villages that may not have direct train connections. They also offer the flexibility to explore multiple destinations in a single day, hopping on and off as you please.

Local Trains: If you're planning to travel between major cities, towns, and popular châteaux within the Loire Valley, local trains are the preferred mode of transportation. The train network covers a wide area and provides efficient connections, making it convenient for day trips or longer journeys.

Trains offer a comfortable and scenic way to travel, allowing you to relax and enjoy the beautiful landscapes as you move between destinations. The train stations are usually centrally located, making it convenient to access nearby attractions and accommodations.

The local train system in the Loire Valley is well-developed, and you'll find regular schedules throughout the day. It's advisable to check the timetables in advance and arrive at the station a few minutes before departure to ensure a smooth journey.

Trains are particularly suitable for visiting major cities like Tours, Orléans, and Angers, as well as the iconic châteaux that are easily accessible by train, such as Château de Chambord, Château de Chenonceau, and Château d'Amboise. They provide a quick and efficient way to travel longer distances, allowing you to maximize your time and explore more attractions within a limited timeframe.

In summary, buses and local trains are both essential components of the public transportation system in the Loire Valley. Buses are ideal for reaching smaller towns, villages, and off-the-beaten-path locations, while trains offer convenient connections between major cities and renowned châteaux. By utilizing these public transportation options, you can efficiently and affordably explore the diverse wonders of the Loire Valley.

Accommodation Options and Recommendations

The Loire Valley offers a wide range of accommodation options to suit various budgets and preferences. From luxurious château hotels to cozy bed and breakfasts, there is something for every type of traveler.

Château Hotels:

For an unforgettable experience, consider staying in one of the charming château hotels scattered throughout the region. These historic properties have been transformed into elegant accommodations, offering a taste of the region's rich heritage.

The Loire Valley is renowned for its magnificent châteaux, and what better way to immerse yourself in the region's history and grandeur than by staying in a château hotel? These unique accommodations provide a truly enchanting experience, combining luxurious amenities with the timeless charm of centuries-old architecture.

Château hotels in the Loire Valley range from grand castles to smaller manor houses, each with its own distinct character and story to tell. Many of these properties have been meticulously restored, preserving their original architectural features while incorporating modern comforts.

As you step inside a château hotel, you'll be greeted by elegant interiors adorned with period furniture, intricate tapestries, and ornate details that harken back to a bygone era. The spacious rooms and suites exude a sense of opulence, often featuring high ceilings, antique furnishings, and lavish decorations.

One of the remarkable aspects of staying in a château hotel is the opportunity to explore the vast grounds and gardens surrounding the property. Imagine strolling through manicured gardens, enjoying peaceful moments by the fountain, or taking in breathtaking views of the rolling countryside. Some château hotels even offer private access to parts of the estate, allowing you to fully immerse yourself in the splendor of the surroundings.

Beyond the architectural marvels and stunning landscapes, château hotels in the Loire Valley offer exceptional hospitality and personalized service. The staff is dedicated to ensuring your stay is memorable, attending to your needs and providing valuable insights about the region. From arranging private tours to recommending local wineries and restaurants, they can help curate a truly bespoke experience tailored to your interests.

Cuisine is another highlight of staying in a château hotel. Many of these properties boast their own fine dining restaurants, where you can savor exquisite French gastronomy paired with exceptional wines from the region. Indulge in gourmet dishes prepared with locally sourced ingredients, showcasing the culinary traditions and flavors of the Loire Valley.

there are several apps and websites available that can help you find and book château hotels in the Loire Valley. Here are a few popular ones:

- Booking.com: Booking.com is a widely used platform that offers a comprehensive range of accommodations, including château hotels. Their user-friendly interface allows you to filter your search based on location, dates, and specific amenities. You can read guest reviews, compare prices, and make reservations directly through the website or the Booking.com mobile app.
- Châteaux & Hôtels Collection: Châteaux & Hôtels Collection is a dedicated hotel collection that specializes in luxury château accommodations in France. They have a website and a mobile app where you can explore their portfolio of château hotels, browse photos, and find detailed information about each property. The app also allows you to book your stay conveniently.
- Relais & Châteaux: Relais & Châteaux is an association of unique luxury hotels and gourmet restaurants around the world. They have a strong presence in the Loire Valley, offering a selection of prestigious château hotels. Their website and mobile app provide a seamless booking experience, showcasing the distinct features and offerings of each property.
- Hôtes Insolites: Hôtes Insolites is a French platform that specializes in unique and unconventional accommodations, including château hotels. Their website and app feature a curated collection of extraordinary properties, allowing you to discover

hidden gems and offbeat château experiences in the Loire Valley.

- TripAdvisor: TripAdvisor is a popular travel website and app that offers a vast range of accommodation options, including château hotels. With millions of user reviews and ratings, it provides valuable insights into the quality and guest experiences of different properties. You can also compare prices, view photos, and make reservations directly through the platform.

When using these apps or websites, be sure to check the specific amenities, services, and policies of each château hotel you're interested in to ensure it aligns with your preferences. It's also recommended to book in advance, especially during peak seasons, to secure your desired dates and room type for a memorable stay in a Loire Valley château hotel.

Whether you're celebrating a special occasion, seeking a romantic getaway, or simply yearning for a one-of-a-kind experience, staying in a château hotel in the Loire Valley is a truly unforgettable choice. It allows you to step back in time and immerse yourself in the region's rich history and cultural heritage, all while enjoying the comforts and luxuries of a top-class hotel. The combination of historic charm, elegant accommodations, impeccable service, and gastronomic delights makes a stay at a château hotel an experience that will leave a lasting impression on your journey through the Loire Valley.

Hotels:

Hotels in the Loire Valley offer a diverse range of options, catering to different budgets and preferences. Whether you're seeking a luxurious stay or a budget-friendly option, you'll find accommodations that suit your needs.

In towns and cities throughout the Loire Valley, you'll discover a variety of hotels, from charming boutique establishments to well-known international chains. These hotels provide comfortable rooms, modern amenities, and often feature unique touches that reflect the region's cultural heritage.

When selecting a hotel in the Loire Valley, it's important to consider its location. Look for accommodations that are centrally located, particularly if you plan to explore multiple attractions in different towns or châteaux. Being in close proximity to the main sights will save you time and make it easier to access the places you wish to visit.

Many hotels in the Loire Valley offer convenient access to the major châteaux and landmarks. They may provide shuttle services, arrange guided tours, or offer bicycle rentals to help you navigate the region. Some hotels even have their own on-site restaurants that showcase the local cuisine and wines, allowing you to savor the flavors of the Loire Valley without venturing far from your accommodation.

In terms of budget, the Loire Valley offers a range of options. You'll find budget-friendly hotels that provide comfortable rooms and essential amenities, perfect for travelers who prioritize affordability without compromising on convenience. These hotels are often located in or near town centers, allowing easy access to dining options, shopping, and local attractions.

For those seeking a more luxurious experience, the Loire Valley boasts a selection of upscale hotels that offer exceptional service, elegant rooms, and additional amenities such as spas, swimming pools, and gourmet restaurants. Some of these hotels are even housed within historical buildings or grand châteaux, adding a touch of opulence and charm to your stay.

To ensure a seamless and enjoyable experience, it's advisable to make reservations in advance, especially during the peak travel season. This guarantees that you secure your preferred hotel and room type, as well as any additional services or special requests you may have.

There are several popular apps and websites that can help you find hotels in the Loire Valley and meet your specific preferences. Here are a few notable ones:

- Booking.com: Booking.com is a widely-used platform that allows you to search and book hotels in the Loire Valley. It offers a comprehensive range of accommodations, from budget-friendly options to luxury hotels. The website and app provide detailed information about each hotel, including guest reviews, photos, and amenities.
- Expedia: Expedia is another popular online travel agency that offers a wide selection of hotels in the Loire Valley. The platform allows you to compare prices, read reviews, and make reservations. Additionally, Expedia often provides deals and discounts, making it a great choice for budget-conscious travelers.
- TripAdvisor: TripAdvisor is a well-known travel website that not only provides hotel listings but also offers traveler reviews, ratings, and recommendations. This can be especially helpful when choosing accommodations in the Loire Valley. The website also provides a forum where users can ask questions and get advice from fellow travelers.

- Hotels.com: Hotels.com is an online booking platform that features an extensive selection of hotels worldwide, including the Loire Valley. The website and app offer user-friendly search filters, allowing you to refine your search based on specific criteria, such as price range, location, and amenities. Hotels.com also has a loyalty program that rewards you with free nights after a certain number of bookings.
- Airbnb: If you prefer a more unique and personalized accommodation experience, Airbnb offers a variety of options in the Loire Valley, including private rooms, apartments, and even entire homes. With Airbnb, you can connect with local hosts and enjoy a more immersive stay, often at competitive prices.

Remember to read reviews, compare prices, and consider the location and amenities offered by each hotel before making a decision. These apps and websites provide a convenient way to search, book, and secure your desired accommodations in the Loire Valley, ensuring a comfortable and enjoyable stay.

By selecting a centrally located hotel that offers easy access to the attractions you wish to visit, you can make the most of your time in the Loire Valley, ensuring a comfortable and convenient base for your explorations.

Bed and Breakfasts:

Bed and Breakfasts, also known as "chambres d'hôtes" in French, offer a unique and charming accommodation option in the Loire Valley. These establishments provide a more intimate and personalized experience for travelers, allowing them to immerse themselves in the local culture and enjoy a warm and welcoming atmosphere.

One of the standout features of bed and breakfasts in the Loire Valley is their cozy and inviting ambiance. The owners of these establishments often open their homes to guests, creating a friendly and familial environment. You can expect personalized attention and hospitality from the hosts, who are usually locals with a deep knowledge of the region. They are often passionate about sharing their insights, recommending hidden gems, and providing valuable tips to make your stay memorable.

The locations of bed and breakfasts are carefully chosen to enhance the overall experience. Many of them are situated in picturesque villages or nestled in the tranquil countryside, offering a peaceful retreat away from the bustling city centers. Staying in a bed and breakfast allows you to appreciate the natural beauty of the Loire Valley, with views of rolling hills, vineyards, or charming village streets right outside your window.

These accommodations are often housed in historic buildings, such as traditional stone houses or converted farmhouses, adding to their unique character and authenticity. The rooms are typically individually decorated, reflecting the personal style and taste of the owners. You can expect comfortable furnishings, cozy beds, and thoughtful touches that create a cozy and homely ambiance.

One of the highlights of staying in a bed and breakfast is the breakfast itself. Each morning, you'll be treated to a delicious and typically homemade breakfast, showcasing local produce and specialties. It's an opportunity to savor regional delicacies, freshly baked bread, homemade jams, local cheeses, and perhaps even some freshly picked fruits from the garden. Breakfast is often served in a communal dining area, allowing you to interact with other guests and share stories and recommendations.

Bed and breakfasts in the Loire Valley offer more than just a place to sleep; they provide a memorable and immersive experience. The hosts are passionate about their region and can provide insider tips on the best nearby attractions, hidden gems, and local events happening during your stay. They may also offer additional services, such as organizing wine tastings, arranging guided tours, or suggesting scenic walking or cycling routes to explore the surroundings.

There are several apps and websites that can help you find and book bed and breakfast accommodations in the Loire Valley or any other destination. Here are a few popular ones:

Airbnb: Airbnb is a well-known platform that offers a wide range of accommodations, including bed and breakfast options. You can search for listings in the Loire Valley, read reviews from previous guests, and communicate directly with hosts to book your stay.

Booking.com: While Booking.com is primarily known for hotel bookings, it also features a selection of bed and breakfasts. The website allows you to filter your search based on location, amenities, and guest ratings to find the perfect B&B for your stay in the Loire Valley.

BedandBreakfast.com: As the name suggests, BedandBreakfast.com is a dedicated platform for finding bed and breakfast accommodations worldwide. You can search specifically for B&Bs in the Loire Valley, read detailed descriptions, view photos, and make reservations directly through the website.

TripAdvisor: TripAdvisor is a popular travel website that provides reviews, recommendations, and bookings for various types of accommodations. You can search for bed and breakfasts in the Loire Valley, read traveler reviews, and compare prices from different booking providers.

Hopper: While Hopper is primarily known as a flight booking app, it also offers a feature called "Hotels Tonight" that allows you to find last-minute deals on accommodations, including bed and breakfasts. This can be a useful option if you're flexible with your travel dates.

When using these apps or websites, it's important to read reviews, check the ratings, and carefully review the listing details to ensure the bed and breakfast meets your preferences and requirements. Additionally, contacting the hosts directly can provide you with more information and help you make an informed decision.

Remember to book your bed and breakfast in advance, especially during peak travel seasons, to secure availability and the best rates.

Whether you're a couple seeking a romantic getaway, a solo traveler in search of authentic experiences, or a family looking for a cozy and welcoming atmosphere, bed and breakfasts in the Loire Valley offer a delightful alternative to traditional hotels. They provide an opportunity to connect with the local culture, enjoy personalized hospitality, and create lasting memories in this enchanting region of France.

Self-Catering Accommodations:

If you prefer more independence and the ability to cook your own meals, renting a vacation home or apartment can be a great option. These self-catering accommodations are available in various sizes and locations, allowing you to immerse yourself in the local lifestyle.

Renting a vacation home or apartment in the Loire Valley provides you with a home away from home. These accommodations are typically fully furnished and equipped with all the necessary amenities, including a kitchen or kitchenette, allowing you to prepare your own meals at your convenience. This option is especially appealing for travelers who enjoy exploring local markets, trying out regional ingredients, and experiencing the culinary delights of the Loire Valley firsthand.

One of the advantages of self-catering accommodations is the flexibility they offer. You can set your own schedule, enjoy leisurely breakfasts in your pajamas, and experiment with cooking traditional French dishes using local produce. It's an opportunity to engage with the region's gastronomic culture in a more intimate and personal way. You can visit local markets, farm stands, and specialty food shops to source fresh ingredients and artisanal products, adding an extra dimension to your travel experience.

Another benefit of self-catering accommodations is the space and privacy they provide. Whether you are traveling with family or friends, renting a vacation home or apartment allows you to have communal spaces to gather and socialize, as well as private areas for relaxation. It offers a more intimate and comfortable environment compared to a hotel room, giving you the freedom to unwind and truly feel at home during your stay.

Self-catering accommodations are available in various sizes and locations throughout the Loire Valley. You can find charming cottages in the countryside, apartments in historic town centers, or even elegant villas with gardens and swimming pools. Depending on your preferences and group size, you can choose the accommodation that best suits your needs. Whether you are seeking a romantic getaway, a family-friendly retreat, or a gathering place for a group of friends, there are options to accommodate everyone.

When considering self-catering accommodations, it is important to research and book in advance, especially during peak travel seasons. Popular areas such as Amboise, Blois, and Saumur tend to have a range of options available, while smaller towns and villages may have more limited choices. It's also a good idea to read reviews and check the amenities and facilities provided to ensure that the rental meets your expectations.

There are several popular online platforms and mobile apps that can help you find and book self-catering accommodations in the Loire Valley and beyond. Here are a few well-known options:

- Airbnb: Airbnb is a widely used platform that connects travelers with local hosts who offer a variety of accommodations, including self-catering options such as entire homes, apartments, or cottages. The platform allows you to search for listings in specific areas, view photos, read reviews from previous guests, and communicate with hosts directly.
- Vrbo (formerly HomeAway): Vrbo is another popular vacation rental platform that offers a wide range of self-catering accommodations, including houses, apartments, and villas. It allows you to search for properties in specific destinations, customize your search based on your preferences, and communicate with property owners or managers.
- Booking.com: While primarily known for hotels, Booking.com also features a selection of self-catering accommodations. You can use the platform to search

for apartments, holiday homes, and other rental properties in the Loire Valley. It provides detailed property descriptions, guest reviews, and a secure booking system.

- TripAdvisor: TripAdvisor is a well-established travel platform that offers a comprehensive range of accommodation options, including self-catering properties. It provides user-generated reviews, ratings, and photos to help you make informed decisions. You can search for vacation rentals, read traveler feedback, and compare prices on the platform.
- Expedia: Expedia is a popular online travel agency that offers a wide array of travel services, including accommodations. It features a selection of self-catering options in the Loire Valley, allowing you to filter your search based on your preferences and book directly through the platform.

When using these apps or platforms, it's important to read the property descriptions, amenities, and guest reviews to ensure that the self-catering accommodation meets your needs and expectations. Additionally, be sure to communicate with the property owner or manager directly if you have any specific questions or requirements.

Remember to book in advance, especially during peak travel seasons, to secure the best options for your stay in the beautiful Loire Valley.

By opting for self-catering accommodations, you can enjoy the freedom, flexibility, and authenticity of living like a local in the Loire Valley. It allows you to create your own unique experiences, discover hidden gems, and truly immerse yourself in the captivating lifestyle of this enchanting region of France.

Camping:

Camping in the Loire Valley is a fantastic option for nature enthusiasts and outdoor adventurers. The region boasts numerous campsites, providing opportunities to immerse yourself in the beautiful landscapes and experience the serene ambiance of the area. Whether you prefer traditional tent camping, have your own camping equipment, or opt for more comfortable accommodations such as cabins or caravans, the Loire Valley offers a range of camping options to suit various preferences and budgets.

Tent Camping: If you enjoy the simplicity and closeness to nature that tent camping provides, the Loire Valley has plenty of campsites equipped with designated spaces for tents. These campsites often offer basic amenities such as toilets, showers, and communal cooking areas. Sleeping under the stars, waking up to the sounds of birds chirping, and enjoying the fresh air are all part of the enchanting camping experience in the Loire Valley.

Cabin Rentals: For those who desire a bit more comfort while still being close to nature, many campsites in the Loire Valley offer cabin rentals. These cabins, often made of wood or other natural materials, provide a cozy and rustic retreat. They are typically equipped with basic amenities such as beds, a small kitchenette, and private bathroom facilities. Cabin rentals offer a balance between the outdoor camping experience and a comfortable sheltered space.

Caravan or RV Camping: If you prefer the convenience of bringing your own accommodation on wheels, the Loire Valley has campsites equipped with spaces for caravans and recreational vehicles (RVs). These campsites often provide electrical hook-ups, water connections, and dumping stations for sewage. Caravan and RV camping allow you to explore the region at your own pace while enjoying the comforts and amenities of your own mobile home.

Campsite Facilities and Activities: Many campsites in the Loire Valley go beyond providing a place to pitch a tent or park a caravan. They often offer a variety of facilities and activities to enhance your camping experience. Common amenities include swimming pools, playgrounds, sports fields, and barbecue areas. Some campsites even organize outdoor activities such as hiking, cycling, fishing, or canoeing, allowing you to fully immerse yourself in the natural beauty of the Loire Valley.

Budget-Friendly Option: Camping in the Loire Valley can be an affordable alternative to traditional accommodations. Campsite fees are generally lower compared to hotels or guesthouses, making it a budget-friendly option for travelers. Additionally, cooking your meals at the campsite can help you save on dining expenses, as many campsites provide communal cooking areas or allow you to use portable grills. Camping allows you to allocate your travel budget towards other experiences, such as exploring the châteaux or indulging in local cuisine.

When planning a camping trip in the Loire Valley, it is advisable to research and book campsites in advance, especially during peak travel seasons, to ensure availability. Consider the location of the campsite in relation to the attractions you wish to visit, as well as the facilities and services offered to ensure they meet your needs and preferences.

There are several mobile apps and websites that can help you find and book campsites in the Loire Valley and beyond. Here are a few popular options:

- Camping World: Camping World is a comprehensive app that allows you to search for campsites worldwide. It provides detailed information about campsites, including amenities, pricing, and user reviews. The app also offers filters to help you find campsites that match your preferences and requirements.
- Pitchup: Pitchup is a camping booking platform that covers a wide range of campsites in various locations, including the Loire Valley. The app allows you to search for campsites based on your desired dates, location, and accommodation preferences. It provides detailed campsite information, reviews, and photos to help you make an informed decision.
- Hipcamp: While primarily focused on camping in the United States, Hipcamp also features a growing number of international campsites, including some in the Loire Valley. The app allows you to search for campsites, glamping sites, and RV parks. It provides information about amenities, activities, and nearby attractions.
- ACSI Campsites Europe: ACSI Campsites Europe is an app specifically designed for camping in Europe. It features an extensive database of campsites, including those in the Loire Valley. The app provides information on campsite facilities, pricing, and user reviews. It also offers offline functionality, allowing you to access campsite information even without an internet connection.

- Camping-app.eu: Camping-app.eu is another app dedicated to finding campsites in Europe. It provides a user-friendly interface with filters to refine your search based on location, facilities, and accommodation types. The app includes campsite descriptions, photos, and reviews to help you choose the right campsite for your needs.

These apps can be downloaded from your mobile device's app store and provide a convenient way to search for and book campsites in the Loire Valley and beyond. Remember to check the availability and book in advance, especially during peak travel seasons, to secure your preferred campsite.

Camping in the Loire Valley offers a unique and immersive way to experience the region's natural beauty, and it allows you to create lasting memories surrounded by picturesque landscapes and the tranquility of the great outdoors.

It is recommended to book your accommodation in advance, especially during the peak season, to secure your preferred choice and ensure availability.

By considering these practicalities and resources, you can effectively plan your trip to the Loire Valley, making the most of your time, transportation options, and finding suitable accommodations that enhance your overall experience in this captivating region of France.

Essential Travel Tips and Safety Information

Health and Safety Precautions

When traveling to the Loire Valley, it's essential to prioritize your health and safety. Here are some important precautions to keep in mind:

Medical Services: It is essential to familiarize yourself with the local medical facilities in the Loire Valley. Research and make a note of the nearest hospitals, clinics, and pharmacies in the areas you plan to visit. In case of an emergency or if you require medical assistance, having this information readily available will be invaluable.

Travel Insurance: Before embarking on your trip to the Loire Valley, consider obtaining comprehensive travel insurance. Look for a policy that covers medical expenses, including emergency medical treatment and evacuation if needed. Additionally, ensure that your insurance plan provides coverage for trip cancellations or interruptions and protects your personal belongings. If you plan to engage in outdoor activities like cycling or hiking, verify if your insurance plan includes coverage for such activities.

Vaccinations: Before traveling to the Loire Valley, consult with your healthcare provider or visit a travel clinic to check if there are any recommended vaccinations for your trip. Ensure that you are up to date on routine vaccinations such as measles, mumps, rubella, diphtheria, tetanus, and pertussis. Depending on your travel plans and the duration of your stay, your healthcare provider may also recommend additional vaccinations such as hepatitis A and B, typhoid, or influenza.

Medications: If you require prescription medications, make sure you have an ample supply to last for the duration of your trip. Keep them in their original packaging, clearly labeled with your name and dosage information. It is also advisable to carry copies of your prescriptions in case you need to refill them during your stay. In addition to your prescribed medications, consider packing a basic first aid kit that includes items such as band-aids, antiseptic ointment, pain relievers, and any specific medications you might need for minor injuries or ailments.

Hygiene and Food Safety: Practicing good hygiene is crucial to stay healthy while traveling in the Loire Valley. Wash your hands frequently, especially before meals, using soap and clean water. If clean water is not readily available, use hand sanitizers that contain at least 60% alcohol. When it comes to drinking water, it is recommended to stick to bottled water or opt for filtered water. When dining out, choose reputable establishments that maintain high hygiene standards. Enjoy the local culinary delights with confidence, but ensure that the food is properly cooked and served hot to minimize the risk of foodborne illnesses.

Sun Protection: The Loire Valley experiences mild to hot summers, and protection from the sun is essential. Wear sunscreen with a high sun protection factor (SPF) to shield your skin from harmful UV rays. Apply sunscreen generously and reapply it frequently, especially after swimming or sweating. Additionally, wear a wide-brimmed hat and sunglasses to protect your face and eyes. Stay hydrated by drinking plenty of water, especially during outdoor activities, to prevent dehydration.

Language and Communication Tips

While English is spoken in some tourist areas, the majority of locals in the Loire Valley primarily speak French. Here are some language and communication tips to enhance your travel experience:

Basic French Phrases:

Learning a few basic French phrases can greatly enhance your interactions with locals and make your travel experience more enjoyable. Here are some essential phrases to consider:

- Greetings: Start your conversations on a friendly note with greetings such as "Bonjour" (Good day), "Bonsoir" (Good evening), or "Salut" (Hi).
- Asking for Directions: When navigating the streets of the Loire Valley, knowing how to ask for directions can be incredibly helpful. You can use phrases like "Excusez-moi, où est la gare?" (Excuse me, where is the train station?) or "Pouvez-vous m'indiquer le chemin vers le château?" (Can you tell me the way to the castle?).
- Ordering Food: Enjoying the culinary delights of the Loire Valley is a must. Use phrases like "Je voudrais un croissant, s'il vous plaît" (I would like a croissant, please) or "Qu'est-ce que vous recommandez?" (What do you recommend?) to explore the local cuisine.
- Expressing Gratitude: Show appreciation by saying "Merci" (Thank you) or "Je vous remercie" (I thank you) when receiving assistance or enjoying a pleasant experience. Adding "beaucoup" (very much) after "merci" emphasizes your gratitude.

Translator Apps:

In addition to learning basic French phrases, technology can also assist you in overcoming language barriers. Translator apps or portable electronic translators can be valuable tools during your travels. These apps can provide translations for both written and spoken language, allowing you to communicate with locals more effectively. Some popular translator apps include Google Translate, Microsoft Translator, and iTranslate.

Politeness and Patience:

Approaching interactions with locals in the Loire Valley with politeness and patience is key to establishing positive connections. Even if you struggle with the language, a smile and a respectful attitude can go a long way. Locals appreciate the effort you make to communicate and will often reciprocate with patience and helpfulness.

English-friendly Establishments:

While learning basic French phrases and using translator apps can be beneficial, it's also helpful to seek out establishments that cater to English-speaking visitors. Tourist information centers, hotels, and restaurants with English-speaking staff can assist you with any inquiries or concerns you may have. They can provide recommendations, offer guidance, and ensure that you have a smooth and enjoyable experience during your stay in the Loire Valley.

Remember, even if language communication is limited, making an effort to connect with locals using basic French phrases, technology, politeness, and patience can lead to meaningful interactions and a deeper appreciation of the local culture.

Cultural Etiquette and Respectful Travel

Dress Code: The Loire Valley is home to numerous churches, cathedrals, and religious sites that hold cultural and historical significance. When visiting these places, it is important to dress modestly and respectfully. Both men and women should avoid wearing revealing or overly casual clothing. It is advisable to carry a shawl or scarf to cover bare shoulders or legs if necessary. By dressing appropriately, you show respect for the religious and cultural values associated with these sites.

Greeting Customs: French people greatly value polite greetings and exchanges, and it is no different in the Loire Valley. When meeting locals or interacting with people in the region, a polite greeting is customary. A simple "Bonjour" (Good day) or "Bonsoir" (Good evening) accompanied by a smile goes a long way in starting conversations on a positive note. Showing respect and acknowledging people with a friendly greeting is appreciated and helps to establish a positive rapport.

Dining Etiquette: The Loire Valley is renowned for its gastronomy, and sharing meals is an integral part of French culture. When dining with locals or in traditional restaurants, it is important to observe local dining customs. Avoid placing your elbows on the table, as this is considered impolite. Wait for the host or hostess to begin the meal before you start eating. Take your time to savor each course and engage in relaxed conversation. Remember to say "Bon appétit" before you begin your meal as a polite gesture.

Tipping: In France, a service charge is typically included in the bill at restaurants and cafes. However, it is customary to leave a small tip, known as "pourboire," for exceptional service. The usual range for tipping is around 5-10% of the total bill. It is customary to leave the tip in cash directly on the table or hand it to the server. Additionally, it is also customary to tip hotel staff, tour guides, and taxi drivers if you are satisfied with their services.

Photography Etiquette: The Loire Valley offers breathtaking landscapes, stunning architecture, and captivating scenes worth capturing in photographs. However, it is important to exercise respect and sensitivity when taking pictures. Before photographing people or private property, always seek permission as a gesture of respect for personal privacy and local customs. In some instances, there may be restrictions on photography, especially in religious sites or private establishments. Pay attention to any signage or instructions provided and follow them accordingly.

By embracing these cultural etiquette tips, you not only show respect for the local customs and traditions but also enhance your own travel experience by fostering positive interactions and understanding with the people of the Loire Valley.

By following these travel tips, you can ensure a safe, enjoyable, and culturally respectful experience during your visit to the Loire Valley.

Conclusion

The Loire Valley is a place that captivates the hearts of all who visit. As you reach the end of your journey through this enchanting region, take a moment to reflect on the unforgettable experiences you have had. From the awe-inspiring châteaux that stand as testaments to centuries of history, to the charming villages that exude rural charm, the Loire Valley has a way of leaving a lasting impression.

Think back to the grandeur of Château de Chambord, with its intricate architectural details and vast grounds that seemingly stretch on forever. Remember the delicate beauty of Château de Chenonceau, gracefully spanning the River Cher and offering glimpses into the lives of past residents. And recall the royal ambiance of Château de Blois, where stories of power, intrigue, and romance are etched into the walls.

But the Loire Valley is more than just its magnificent châteaux. It's a region where gastronomy takes center stage, where you savored exquisite wines and indulged in mouthwatering delicacies. It's a place where you discovered the joy of participating in local festivals, immersing yourself in the vibrant traditions and cultural heritage of the area. And it's a destination where nature flourishes, from the serene Loire River that meanders through the landscape to the meticulously maintained gardens and parks that invite peaceful contemplation.

As you bid farewell to the Loire Valley, let it be the beginning of a lifelong love affair with travel. Allow the memories and experiences from this journey to inspire future adventures, whether within the borders of France or across the globe. The Loire Valley has shown you the power of history, the beauty of nature, and the warmth of local hospitality. Carry these lessons with you as you continue to explore and discover new destinations.

In the end, the Loire Valley will always hold a special place in your heart. Its magic will continue to resonate within you, reminding you of the moments of awe, joy, and wonder you experienced. Embrace the memories, cherish the reflections, and let the spirit of the Loire Valley guide you towards new horizons, fueling your passion for travel and the pursuit of extraordinary experiences.

Farewell, dear traveler, and may your future adventures be as extraordinary as your journey through the magical Loire Valley.

Useful apps and Websites

When visiting the Loire Valley, here are 15 useful apps and websites that can enhance your travel experience:

Loire Valley Tourism Official Website (www.loirevalley-france.co.uk):

The official tourism website for the Loire Valley is a valuable resource for visitors. It provides comprehensive information on attractions, accommodations, events, and practical tips. You can explore different regions within the Loire Valley, such as Tours, Amboise, and Orleans, and discover their unique offerings. The website offers insights into the famous châteaux, picturesque villages, natural landscapes, and cultural activities that make the Loire Valley a captivating destination. It also provides information on transportation options, including trains, buses, and car rentals, making it easier to plan your itinerary.

Google Maps (www.google.com/maps):

Google Maps is a reliable navigation app that offers detailed maps, directions, and real-time traffic information, making it an essential tool for navigating the Loire Valley. Whether you're driving, walking, or using public transportation, Google Maps can guide you to your desired destinations. You can search for specific attractions, restaurants, or accommodations and get accurate directions to reach them. The app also provides information about nearby points of interest, such as parks, shopping areas, and landmarks, allowing you to explore the surrounding areas easily.

TripAdvisor (www.tripadvisor.com):

TripAdvisor is a popular platform for reading reviews, finding recommendations, and booking accommodations, restaurants, and attractions in the Loire Valley. You can browse through a wide range of traveler reviews and ratings to make informed decisions about where to stay, dine, and visit. The website also features forums where you can ask questions and get advice from fellow travelers or locals who have already visited the Loire Valley. Additionally, you can book accommodations, reserve tables at restaurants, and purchase tickets for attractions directly through the website.

Loire Valley Wine Official Website (www.loirevalleywine.com):

For wine enthusiasts, the Loire Valley Wine official website is a treasure trove of information. It allows you to explore the world of Loire Valley wines, learn about different wine-producing regions, vineyards, and grape varieties. The website provides details about wine routes and suggested itineraries, helping you plan wine tasting experiences and visits to wineries. You can also find information about wine-related events, festivals, and workshops taking place in the region. Whether you're a novice or a connoisseur, this website will deepen your appreciation for the exquisite wines of the Loire Valley.

Michelin Travel (www.viamichelin.com):

Michelin Travel is a useful website and app for planning road trips, finding the best routes, and discovering scenic drives in the Loire Valley. It offers detailed maps, driving directions, and suggested itineraries, allowing you to customize your journey. The website also provides information on points of interest, including attractions, viewpoints, and picnic spots along the way. Michelin Travel helps you optimize your travel time, choose the most scenic routes, and explore the hidden gems of the Loire Valley.

Loire Châteaux Official Website (www.loire-chateaux.org):

The Loire Châteaux official website is dedicated to providing detailed information about the various châteaux in the Loire Valley. It offers insights into their history, architectural features, and notable highlights. You can find information about opening hours, ticket prices, and special events happening at each château. The website also suggests itineraries for visiting multiple châteaux in a day, allowing you to make the most of your time. Whether you're interested in the grandeur of Château de Chambord, the elegance of Château de Chenonceau, or the historical significance of Château de Blois, this website will guide you through the enchanting world of Loire Valley châteaux.

Weather.com or a Weather App:

Staying updated on the weather conditions in the Loire Valley is crucial for planning your activities and packing appropriately. Websites like Weather.com or weather apps provide reliable forecasts, current weather conditions, and temperature trends. They can help you decide when to visit outdoor attractions, go for a hike, or plan a picnic, ensuring that you make the most of your time in the region.

Velovelo (www.velovelo.com):

If you're interested in exploring the Loire Valley on two wheels, Velovelo is a dedicated website for cycling routes and bike rental services. It provides information about cycling itineraries, including distance, difficulty level, and scenic highlights. You can find recommendations for cycling loops, family-friendly routes, and off-the-beaten-path trails. The website also offers resources on bike rentals, repair shops, and cycling-friendly accommodations, making it easier to plan your cycling adventure in the Loire Valley.

Loire à Vélo Official Website (www.loireavelo.fr):

The Loire à Vélo official website is specifically designed for those interested in the renowned Loire à Vélo cycling route. This route spans over 800 kilometers along the Loire River, offering a scenic and enjoyable cycling experience. The website provides detailed information on cycling itineraries, services, and accommodations along the route. You can discover charming towns, vineyards, and natural landscapes as you pedal through the Loire Valley. Whether you're a seasoned cyclist or a leisure rider, this website will assist you in planning and navigating the Loire à Vélo route.

Trainline (www.thetrainline.com):

Trainline is a handy app for checking train schedules, booking tickets, and managing your train travel within the Loire Valley and to/from other regions. It provides real-time updates on train timetables, platform information, and ticket prices. You can conveniently book your train tickets in advance, saving time and ensuring a smooth journey.

Trainline also offers mobile ticket options, allowing you to have your tickets readily accessible on your smartphone.

Uber or Local Taxi Apps:

For convenient and on-demand transportation within cities or for shorter distances in the Loire Valley, ride-hailing apps like Uber or local taxi apps can be incredibly useful. With these apps, you can easily request a ride, track the driver's location, and pay through the app. They provide a convenient alternative to public transportation, particularly for reaching specific destinations or traveling during late hours when other transport options might be limited.

French Phrasebook or Translation App:

While English is spoken in many tourist areas of the Loire Valley, carrying a French phrasebook or using translation apps like Google Translate can greatly enhance your communication with locals. These resources help you understand basic French phrases, order food, ask for directions, and engage in simple conversations. They bridge the language barrier and show your effort to connect with the local culture and people.

Currency Converter App:

If you're traveling from a different currency zone, a currency converter app can be invaluable for quickly converting prices and managing your expenses. These apps provide up-to-date exchange rates and allow you to calculate the equivalent value of items in your home currency. This helps you make informed decisions while shopping, dining, and budgeting during your trip to the Loire Valley.

Park4Night (www.park4night.com):

For campers or motorhome travelers, Park4Night is an ideal website and app that provides information about campsites, parking spots, and overnight stays in the Loire Valley. It offers a database of recommended spots, including official campsites, wild camping areas, and parking areas suitable for overnight stays. The app includes user reviews, photos, and facilities available at each location, making it easier to find suitable spots for your camping adventure.

Loiretourisme (www.loiretourisme.com):

Loiretourisme is a comprehensive website that offers information about tourist activities, events, and attractions in the Loire Valley, with a particular focus on the Loiret department. It provides insights into cultural festivals, exhibitions, and local celebrations happening during your visit. The website also highlights lesser-known attractions, offbeat experiences, and hidden gems in the Loire Valley. Whether you're interested in history, nature, or gastronomy, Loiretourisme helps you discover the diverse offerings of the region.

By utilizing these apps and websites, you'll have access to valuable information, convenient navigation, and personalized recommendations that will enhance your travel experience in the beautiful Loire Valley.

Remember to download and familiarize yourself with these apps and websites before your trip to ensure you have access to all the necessary information and resources while exploring the beautiful Loire Valley.